BETTING
ON
MYSELF

To Mildred & Bill,

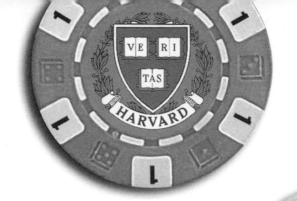

BETTING
ON
MYSELF

STEVEN CRIST

*Adventures of a Horseplayer
and Publisher*

DRF Press
NEW YORK

Published by
Daily Racing Form Press
100 Broadway, 7th Floor
New York, NY 10005

ISBN: 0-9726401-0-X

Library of Congress Control Number: 2003100926

Cover and jacket designed by Chris Donofry
Text design by Neuwirth and Associates, Inc.

Printed in the United States of America

TABLE OF CONTENTS

BETTING
ON
MYSELF

GOING TO THE DOGS

T WAS A WARM spring evening in Cambridge, Massachusetts, in May of 1977 when my friend George Meyer made the fateful suggestion:

"Let's go to Wonderland."

George and I were sitting on a bench in Harvard Square, a pair of longhaired college students with no plans for the evening or the rest of our lives. We were just finishing up our junior years at Harvard College, and a final irresponsible summer awaited us. We were editors of *The Harvard Lampoon*, the college's humor magazine, and we had somehow talked a New York publishing house into a $5,000 advance for an anthology called *The Big Book of College Life*.

We had spent half the money renting a vacationing professor's six-bedroom house for the staff, paid ourselves and six others a $200 advance, and figured that what was left over would keep us all in beer and groceries for the rest of the summer. We also knew we could wait until August to do any serious work on the book.

I didn't know Wonderland was a racetrack. I didn't even know that a horse named Seattle Slew was about to complete a sweep of the Triple Crown, and I'm not sure it had registered four years earlier when Secretariat had done the same. A year from graduation, I had no idea what I wanted to do for a living, but horse racing seemed as unlikely a career choice as training elephants.

I had enjoyed a happy and privileged childhood growing up in an apartment overlooking the Hudson River on the Upper West Side of Manhattan and attended the same nearby private school for 12 years. I was the only child of two professionally successful parents, my mother a well-known movie critic, my father the head of his own public-relations firm. Our home was frequently filled with their friends who worked at newspapers, and everyone smoked cigarettes, drank martinis, and made clever remarks.

The two things I really enjoyed doing were compiling baseball statistics and playing the piano. With my parents out at movie and theater premieres several nights a week, I developed an obsessive devotion to a board game called Strat-O-Matic, a baseball simulation that to this day has a cult following. Each major-league player had a card reflecting his detailed statistics for the previous season. Rolling three dice for each turn at bat approximated the likely results and, over time, closely replicated the statistics of each player.

I would play entire 162-game seasons at my desk among all-star teams plucked from the cards, and my favorite part was being the scorekeeper, recording each at-bat on official score sheets. In addition to memorizing thousands of players' statistics, I developed an unconscious fluidity at calculating percentages. I was less interested in the outcome of individual games than in crowning my own league leaders. It became second nature to me that a batter who started the season with 24 hits in 84 at-bats was a .287 hitter.

Playing the piano came just as easily, and by the time I was 15 I had gotten a weekend job as the intermission piano player for the Roy Eldridge sextet at Jimmy Ryan's Dixieland Club on 52nd Street's Jazz Row. Customers would send cocktails up to the kid at the piano, and the owner, fearful of losing his liquor license, would pour them out and send me across the street to the penny arcade to stay out of trouble until my next set.

Around the time of Secretariat, I fell under the spell of a high-school English teacher who introduced me to the works of T. S. Eliot and James Joyce and pretty much convinced me that the most important thing in life was to study great literature and hope that someday I would be worthy of writing poetry or novels. So I went off to Harvard to be an English major, fully expecting to move from undergraduate to master's to doctoral studies.

The problem was, a year from college graduation, I had grown to hate the study of literature. I felt as if I were serving a jail sentence sitting in the gloomy stacks of Harvard's majestic Widener Library, trying to slog through the canon of great books. I might as well have been reading a foreign language. I felt no connection with anything written more than 100 years ago. I agreed with the notion that someone should preserve these books and teach them to future generations, but I knew that person shouldn't be me.

Not that any of this had stopped me from being considered a promising academic prospect. The secret of Harvard was that getting in was the most difficult part; once you were there, you didn't really have to work very hard. I could do well in courses by writing glib papers about the literature without reading or understanding it, merely by debating philosophical and critical issues that others had raised.

This charade was about to continue because I was scheduled to spend my senior year writing a thesis on the particularly obscure topic I had made my area of expertise. "The Influence of the Seventeenth Century Metaphysical Poets on the Eighteenth Century Satirists" was supposed to be my ticket to graduate school. My prospects seemed a choice between that and playing the piano in bars, but I knew music was a tough way to make a living. Pianists with far more talent than I were turning gray and still working Holiday Inns.

So I suppose I was ready for something new, not just that May evening but in general, when George Meyer suggested we spend an evening at Wonderland Greyhound Park, the last stop on Boston's Blue Line subway. I had only taken the Blue Line as far as the airport, and never even noticed the names of two of the stops past Logan: Suffolk Downs and Wonderland.

George bought us a couple of Wonderland programs at the Harvard Square newsstand and as we rode the train he shared his entire racetrack knowledge, gleaned from childhood trips to a dog track near where he'd grown up in Tucson, Arizona. There was no dog racing in New York. It flourished in just a few pockets of the country, such as New England, Florida, and the Southwest.

Each race had eight dogs and it was your job to figure out the winner of the race, and sometimes the second- and third-place finishers as well. The key, George explained to me, was in reading something called the past performances, a kind of shorthand numeric code that told you about a dog's recent races. The inside front cover of the Wonderland program explained the symbols and their meaning under the headline "The Program—Man's 2nd Best Friend":

"The program is the handicapper's most valuable tool. Difficult as it may look, it is relatively simple to read. It is merely a statistical summary of each greyhound along with a brief analysis of his last seven performances. Breaking it down may provide the razor's edge you need."

Each horizontal line told the story of a single race with a series of numbers and abbreviations:

5-29-6 5-16 F 31.62 73 5 5 4 3 1-1 4.00 A With rush outs.

This translated to mean that this dog had raced on May 29 in the sixth race; the race had been five-sixteenths of a mile long; the track was fast that night; the winner's time was 31.62 seconds; the dog's weight at post time was 73 pounds; the dog had started from the fifth post position; he had been fifth early, moved up to fourth, was third at the top of the stretch, and crossed the finish line first, by one length; he went off at odds of 4-1; the race had been a Grade "A" event; and he had won with a "rush" on the outside of the track.

Sitting there on the Blue Line, reading my first set of past performances, something clicked. As much as the English literature of 250 years ago seemed written in an impenetrable foreign tongue, this was like hearing a new language but understanding it right away. Each line told a simple and compact little story, entirely factual and without exaggeration, and you could absorb it at a glance without stopping to parse each element. After years of constructing convoluted theories about seventeenth-century poets and eighteenth-century satirists, I had found something that was pure and straightforward and utterly without fakery.

When I had fallen for the idea of a life of literature by reading James Joyce's *A Portrait of the Artist as a Young Man,* I had become entranced by his notion of an "epiphany," a moment in life when you make an instantaneous realization that connects your solitary soul to the world at large. It sounded like a wonderful thing and I felt inadequate for never having had one. I had thought that if I ever did have an epiphany, I would find it in the pages or notes of some lofty work of culture. But you don't get to pick your epiphanies, and my first one had instead come in the past-performance lines of a dog-track program.

It was as if the mathematical portion of my brain had been suddenly reawakened after years of denial. My childhood facility for arithmetic, enhanced and nurtured by those desktop Strat-O-Matic seasons, had also always had a more bothersome side. I had several small and useless arithmetic compulsions, such as multiplying the squares of 2 up to eight digits and mentally re-alphabetizing words—I saw *metaphysical* as *aacehilmpsty* and turned *wonderland* into *addelnnorw.* This brain tic was useful for playing Scrabble but otherwise was an inescapable ringing in my ears. The past performances fully absorbed me and silenced the clatter, something the great poets had never done.

I had suppressed these mental buzzings as much as possible and considered them some sort of aberration, since I had always been told I was a word person rather than a number person. My high school in New York City, eager to boast acceptances at prestigious Ivy League colleges, had packaged me as an offbeat, artsy type—*His grades are nothing special, but he's the editor of the school paper and plays the piano at jazz clubs.* There was mild panic in the guidance office when my SAT scores came in—only respectable on the verbal section but nearly perfect at math. A guidance counselor actually suggested I retake the tests and perhaps miss a few math questions next time to present a more consistent profile to college admissions offices.

When George and I got to Wonderland, the math matched right up with the scene. I had been to county fairs with harness races as a child, but the quarter-mile dog track and the sleek hounds in their color-coded blankets were like an intricate miniature, a slot-racing set-up with dogs instead of little cars. The broad apron sloping toward the track was filled with men intently studying the past-performance lines, occasionally glancing up at the blinking odds boards. The dogs were being walked up and down the track as festive military marching music played briskly in the background. Where had this been all my life?

Now came the best part. I had been torn between the merits of two dogs, numbers 1 and 8, both of whom had won their last races by several lengths in faster times than tonight's opponents. George had explained a bet called the quinella, where you bet on two dogs and collected if they ran first and second in either order. I stepped to the window and passed the first two dollars of my life through a parimutuel window, betting a 1-8 quinella.

The 1 dog shot to the front under his red blanket and took a commanding lead into the first turn as the 8 dog steadily advanced in his black-and-gold colors from the outside.

Turning for home, the two of them were clear of the pack and the 8 caught the 1 at the wire. The 1-8 quinella paid $16.80 and I was $14.80 ahead for life. I don't know if I actually spoke the fateful four words that every lucky beginner says upon cashing his first bet, a phrase guaranteed to tempt the deities of wagering to reward you with a lifetime of parimutuel heartache, but I sure thought them:

What an easy game.

WHEN GEORGE AND I got back to the rented *Lampoon* house that night, we immediately turned to the advance programs we had bought for the next night's racing. We spent the rest of the summer that way, handicapping the dog races from midnight until nearly dawn, sleeping until early afternoon, waking up to handicap some more, and then boarding the Blue Line as twilight fell. Soon we had accumulated a tower of Wonderland programs, which carried not only each night's past performances but also the previous night's result charts, giving us plenty of data to test out our primitive handicapping systems and theories.

On paper, we tried every automatic system we could think of against hundreds of results, attempting to discover the secret of beating the game: betting the dog with the fastest time, or the highest win percentage, or the favorite, or the two favorites in the quinella. Nothing worked. It might not be such an easy game after all—unless Downing or Rooster Cogburn was running.

Unlike horses, greyhounds race up to twice a week and under identical rather than varying conditions. In Thoroughbred racing, it was considered spectacular when Cigar won 16 straight races from 1994 through 1996, but plenty of greyhounds have done that over the years, and one named JJ Doc Richard reeled off 37 in a row in 1995. In the summer of 1977, Wonderland's king was Rooster Cogburn, who was simply a few lengths better than anyone at the track. As his winning streak grew, he became an item on the Boston sports pages and talk began of a possible best-of-three match-race series against a similarly successful dog named Downing, who was winning everything in Florida.

Downing won the first matchup down in Florida but Rooster had gotten off to a slow start. They came north to Wonderland for the rematch and that night we were pure fans, rooting for the pride of Wonderland against the invader. It wasn't close. Downing, a massive creature who looked as if he could eat or trample anything he couldn't outrun, blasted to the lead and Rooster never got close. We were humbled, but in racing you're allowed to change your loyalties. Downing stayed at Wonderland and we were his biggest fans as he repeatedly destroyed Rooster Cogburn and any other dog Wonderland could field.

Downing would have to fall down to lose a race and maybe fall down twice to finish worse than third. He would routinely pay $2.20 to show, then the Massachusetts state minimum payoff on a $2 bet. We would watch him with proprietary pride but not bet. With rarely more than $20 or $30 in our pockets, why even bother betting $20 to win $2? We fantasized about having access to bigger money. If you had $500 to bet on him, it was the easiest $50 you could ever make.

At some point one of us realized we did have access to that much money—the remainder of the *Lampoon* book advance. It would be so easy to cash a check, bet on Downing to show, and put the $500 back in the bank the next morning. So we tried it, but we got greedy. Downing usually paid $2.60 or $2.80 to win—paltry payoffs, but three or four times as much profit as we could get from our super-safe show bets.

So we decided to switch from betting him to show to betting him to win, and he picked that night to collide with another dog coming out of the starting box. He regained his balance and took off again, launching an incredible rally, but could only get up for third. Instead of winning the world's easiest $50, we had lost $500 in less than 31 seconds.

Rooster Cogburn was running later that night and looked like a cinch, but there was no way to get back the $500 by betting him to win. So we changed strategy. Instead of betting a lot to win a little, we would try to do the reverse. We decided to attack the trifecta, a bet in which you have to pick the first three finishers in order. In an eight-dog race, there are only eight possible winners but there are 336 different possible trifecta combinations from 1-2-3 through 8-7-6. The trifecta routinely paid in the hundreds, sometimes more than $1,000.

The bet was a lot easier if you assumed Rooster was going to win—now there were only 42 possible combinations of who could finish second and third behind him. For $84, we could buy every $2 trifecta with Rooster on top. We would lose money if logical favorites ran second or third, but maybe we could get a longshot to hit the board.

We were hoping and rooting for chaos, and we got it. Rooster won easily and longshots somehow clunked up for second and third, triggering a trifecta payoff that almost got us even for Downing's earlier loss. We thanked the deities of the dog track and the experience scared us enough that the bank account went untouched thereafter.

As our increasingly resentful colleagues wrote their pieces for the book and enjoyed a lazy summer in Boston, George and I ignored the project until the week before it was due. We would coax friends into joining us for a trip to the end of the

Blue Line, and they would pretend to be entertained and mildly amused, but had no interest in a return visit.

No one could understand the depth of our devotion to this new hobby, and I don't think I understood it myself. I wasn't making money or friends at the track, but I was serenely happy being there. It wasn't just an escape from the real world, but an escape to something challenging and fascinating where I felt completely comfortable.

We finally had to have someone drive us to a hotel far from the Blue Line and strand us there for a week with two electric typewriters and several bottles of No-Doz to get the book done. We finished with about an hour to spare, and promptly resumed our Wonderland trips as senior year began.

That fall, we expanded our reach and found other dog tracks within an hour of Boston—Taunton and Raynham in Massachusetts, and Seabrook, just over the New Hampshire border and down the road from New England's biggest nuclear power plant. We didn't have cars (a city boy, I didn't even know how to drive), but there were $1 chartered buses to these tracks. We had tried Boston's horse track, Suffolk Downs, a couple of times but felt completely out of our element. We had come to think we knew something about dog racing, and there were plenty of greyhound tracks running day and night to keep us busy.

Seabrook offered an irresistible deal. On Saturdays they ran tripleheaders, with 12 races starting at 10:00 A.M., 12 more in the afternoon, and a final dozen at night. How could we pass up 36 dog races in a day? We learned just how long a tripleheader day could be the first time we went and lost all our money by the seventh race on the morning program. We were marooned there another 12 hours until the bus returned to Boston.

Early that fall on a trip home to New York, I decided it was time to tell my parents about my new hobby and my loss of interest in continuing to explore the influence of the Metaphysical poets on Alexander Pope. They didn't seem too disappointed that graduate school was probably not in my future, and my father actually proposed that we make an outing to Belmont Park. On the drive there, he told me how, as a young man, he had been seduced by some betting system, lost a lot more than he could afford, and had never bet more than $2 a race since then. Still, he said, a day at the track could be a lot of fun and it was time for me to see what a real racetrack looked like.

Belmont was stunning, an enormous green park with a massive racing oval six times the circumference of a dog track. Everything was Wonderland on a vastly inflated scale, from the size of the animals and the crowd all the way to the equivalent of the Wonderland program: In horse racing there was an entire daily newspaper, something called the *Daily Racing Form*, which had news stories and statistics wrapped around past performances quite similar to those for the dogs.

We arrived late but had unwittingly picked a good day. The featured race was the Futurity Stakes for 2-year-olds, the fourth meeting in a budding rivalry between two colts named Affirmed and Alydar. My father came back from the window and showed me his $2 win ticket on Affirmed. I told him we were on the same horse, neglecting to add that I had bet $20.

The race was a thriller, nip and tuck to the wire, and Affirmed prevailed by a nose. I was happy to collect $44 but felt as if I had made a narrow escape. Alydar, who had surged from off the pace to take a narrow lead before being outnodded at the wire, had won my affection. He seemed flashier, more gallant for having to make up ground. Surely, as the races got longer between now and the Kentucky Derby eight months later, his acceleration would allow him to mow down the uninteresting, one-paced front-runner Affirmed.

Five weeks later, my opinion was vindicated when I made my second trip to Belmont and Alydar blew past Affirmed to win the one-mile Champagne Stakes by a length and a quarter. I bet back the $44 I had won on Affirmed in the Futurity, the largest win bet I had ever made except for the embezzled $500 on Downing the night he lost, and collected $110. Fortunately, their next meeting took place two weeks later in Maryland on my 21st birthday, so I was unable to lose my $110 when Affirmed won the Laurel Futurity by a neck.

Back in Boston, George and I continued to take the subway to Wonderland or the bus to Seabrook several times a week as it began to seem real that I would have to decide what to do after graduating in a few months. I finally had to tell my thesis adviser, a gray-haired, motorcycle-riding professor of English named John Bullitt, that I no longer cared about the Metaphysicals and the satirists. He asked me what I did care about, and it all came spilling out about Wonderland and Downing and now Affirmed and Alydar.

"Why don't you try writing about that?" he suggested.

That had never occurred to me. Writing had once seemed natural and fun, but had become synonymous with drudgery in the service of academia. Maybe it would be different if I enjoyed the subject. I wrote to every magazine I could find on the Harvard Square newsstand, proposing an article about the fascinating, little-known world of greyhound racing in Massachusetts. Most ignored me but *Boston* magazine agreed to take a look. Five thousand words and $500 later, I was technically a professional racing writer.

Unfortunately, I had now exhausted the possibilities of being paid to write about dog racing, and graduation was drawing near. Using my *Boston* magazine piece as my only published "clip," I applied for an entry-level job at every newspaper and magazine in New York and Boston and went on half a dozen interviews, which were followed by weeks of silence.

The first Saturday in May, Affirmed and Alydar met for the first time since the Laurel Futurity. They had both been dominant winning their prep races while avoiding each other, and Alydar was a slight favorite at 6-5. Maybe in lieu of a job, I could bet on horses. I put $200 on Alydar and watched in horror as Affirmed held him off to win the Kentucky Derby.

Two days later, the phone rang in my Cambridge dorm room. It was *The New York Times,* offering me a job as a night copyboy on one condition: I had to start by the end of the week. I still had exams to take later in the month and I had no idea what a night copyboy was, but it was the only prospect I had. Moving to New York meant no more dog racing, but maybe it was time to move up to the horses. I took the job on the spot and reported for work that Friday.

My workday would begin at 7:00 P.M. and end at 3:00 A.M., which sounded perfect to me. I was a night owl who hadn't gotten up before noon in years, and had ridden the subways alone in the middle of the night since I was a teenager coming home from Jimmy Ryan's. Also, this meant my afternoons would now be free to go to the races at Belmont.

GETTING A JOB at the mighty *New York Times* sounded impressive to others, but I had grown up in a household that liked the so-called paper of record about as little as I liked Affirmed.

My mother, Judith Crist, had been a reporter, editor, and finally a movie critic for the *Times's* rival, *The New York Herald Tribune.* In a time when New York had seven daily newspapers, the Sundays of my childhood were spent surrounded by piles of newsprint and hearing my parents knock the *Times*, which they considered unimaginatively written and edited, the boring and pompous lapdog of big business. The *Tribune*, I was taught, was a writers' paper with a keener eye and a more liberal point of view. The *Times* called everyone "Mr.," even in its small and sober sports section.

Several newspaper strikes in the 1960's, coupled with the increasing popularity of television news, had ended the great daily-newspaper era in New York. Three of the papers, already the survivors of previous mergers—the *Herald Tribune*, the *Journal American*, and the *World-Telegram and Sun*—were forced to merge into one *World Journal Tribune* (known as the Widget), and within a year it too was gone. Now only the corporate *Times* and two tabloids, the blue-collar *Daily News* and the then-liberal *New York Post*, were left.

Yet even as newspapers were struggling and shutting down, journalism, long considered a slightly disreputable profession, was becoming a hugely popular and ever more serious career path. *All the President's Men*, the book and subsequent movie about *The Washington Post* and Watergate, had elevated the popular image of newspaper reporters from scandal-seeking ferrets to good-looking and patriotic heroes saving the republic. Earnest young do-gooders on college campuses who a decade earlier wanted to join the Peace Corps now aspired to be journalists. It infuriated my fellow graduating seniors who had toiled on the terribly serious campus newspaper, *The Harvard Crimson*, that the only *Times* hire from the class had been a *Lampoon* guy whose primary daily reading material was the Wonderland track program.

I was walking into the *Times* at a moment of technical as well as societal transition. My first month was the paper's last month of being published the way it had been for decades, through the mechanical marvel of "hot type." I worked in the main newsroom, which had three primary areas, for the local or "metro" desk, the national desk, and the foreign desk. The sports and arts departments and the Sunday sections such as the book review were located elsewhere in the building, far from the news nexus.

Reporters and rewrite men would bat out their stories on manual typewriters, and as they completed each page they would yell "Copy!" The copyboys, six of us, sat on a long wooden bench and it was our job to run to the reporter's desk, take his page, and stuff it into a pneumatic-tube system that would whisk it to the composing room, where old men in inky aprons retyped the stories on a machine that manufactured lines of metal type. They would then run off a copy of the typeset story, send it back by pneumatic tube, and we ran these "proofs" to the various editors' desks for corrections and changes.

When I got to work each night at 7:00, the newsroom would be at its busiest, and no sooner had you sat down from your most recent sprint to the pneumatic tube than you were at the head of the bench again, poised for another run. Things calmed down after the first edition went out around 9:00 P.M., and after the late edition went to bed around 11:00, only the two newest hires, working the graveyard shift, stayed on.

After midnight, there were two jobs: fetching beer from the all-night delicatessen across the street for the late-night editors, and "sweeping the desks"—rolling up every scrap of paper, phone message, and scribbled-on napkin on every desk in the newsroom in massive sheets of raw newsprint, loading the huge balls into shopping carts, and wheeling them to a vast storage room. This was the *Times*'s way of preserving the record of what had gone into every story should someone file a lawsuit.

Late on my first night on the job, an editor on the foreign desk hollered me over and gave me a dollar to go across the street and buy him a bottle of Heineken, which at the time cost 90 cents. I returned and set down his beer and his change near his elbow, and without looking up or saying a word he slowly pushed the dime back in my direction with a single fingertip. I stood there paralyzed, wondering if this was a test or a gratuity. This was a little bit of a comedown after betting $200 on Alydar to win the Derby a week earlier. I walked away pretending not to notice the dime and the editors started laughing.

"They must be paying the copyboys a lot better these days," said one.

It turned out that nearly everyone in the newsroom had broken in as a copyboy, even the boss, Abe Rosenthal. He was now the executive editor, the ultimate editorial decision-maker, reporting only to the Sulzberger family, which owned the paper and confined its editorial influence to deciding which political candidates to endorse.

Rosenthal called me in for a brief audience after I had been working there for a week, and explained what being a copyboy was really about. If I wanted to be a reporter, I should start coming up with ideas for stories and pestering the editors to let me try writing one. I wouldn't get a byline but I might get noticed around the building and get paid up to $50 a story.

I had no idea where to start. All I knew about being a reporter was what I had overheard around the house growing up and the editing I'd gotten on the *Boston* magazine piece on Wonderland, but it didn't look that difficult. There was a refreshing simplicity about it after years of constructing delib-erately ambiguous essays about long-dead poets. This was so much more direct and honest, like the past performances. All you had to do was talk to people, collect the facts, and lay them out with only enough writerly interference to hold the reader's interest.

Now all I needed was something to write about. The sports department had people covering Affirmed and Alydar, and the dogs were a tough sell in a state that had not staged a greyhound race since the 1930's.

I had learned quickly that people who work until 3:00 A.M. do not rush home to be in bed by 3:30. The late editors would go off drinking and the two late copyboys were often invited along. Sometimes you all ended up at an after-hours club for a few rounds, and on one of those nights someone offered to sell me a bag of pot for $300. Back in college, the going price had been $80. Maybe I had a story.

I started calling drug-prevention agencies out of the phone book and asking them why marijuana had gotten so expensive. I learned that the drug's potency as well as its price had quadrupled in a few years' time, and it was a pretty interesting story of how oversupply of the old stuff had led growers to develop new and more expensive strains.

I took my findings to the metro-desk editors and they were ecstatic. This was exactly the kind of story they loved, though not necessarily for the right reasons. The proper and respectful *Times* was desperately unhip, the shiny-shoed federal agent trying to blend in at the party and usually failing miserably. Now one of their informants had actually infiltrated the subculture and they had a scoop. The story was considered for page 1 and ended up on the coveted front page of the second section.

The stronger-pot story opened doors for me everywhere in the newsroom. The metro desk would wake me at home almost every morning now with an assignment to do before working the graveyard shift. They were mostly dismal errands beneath the dignity of the real reporters—asking people in the subway on a sweltering day whether it was hot enough for them, in hopes of producing a colorful quote for someone else's story on the heat wave; attending fringe-group protest marches; sitting through public hearings on zoning or sewage proposals on the slim chance something newsworthy might be said.

A month of it was probably worth two years of journalism school. Most days I would report back to the office with my quotes or news and sit with a reporter or editor and turn it into a story. Occasionally, if it was close to deadline, I would instead call the "recording room," where you spoke into a tape recorder and someone would play back what you dictated and type it up. I learned quickly how to turn a day's legwork into a smooth narrative, to compose a story in my head as I dictated, and to get things right the first time because there were no second chances.

I was so busy that I had no time to fulfill my notion of spending afternoons at Belmont learning about horse racing. Although I was taking home only a $157 weekly paycheck, I was living rent-free at my parents' apartment while trying to save up a deposit for my own place and managed to divert another $200 to bet on Alydar in the Belmont Stakes. I got the day off from work and took the train out to Belmont, where I joined 65,416 other people in watching one of the greatest stretch duels in history.

I didn't have a seat and had to jump up in the crowd behind the reserved seats to get glimpses of the race. Alydar, who had run out of ground to catch Affirmed in the Derby and Preakness, drew even and got a head in front in midstretch of the Belmont. Finally! But the next time I jumped up, Affirmed had battled back from the inside, and he poked his nose in front to win the Triple Crown. I knew I had seen something important, but winning the Triple Crown seemed like no big deal—Seattle Slew had done it the year before, Secretariat five years earlier. As I write this 25 years later, it has not happened since.

NEW YORK DIDN'T have dog racing but it did have something called OTB. Facing a huge budget crisis in 1971, New York had become the first state to legalize offtrack betting and there were now more than 100 betting shops around the city, including one a few blocks from my parents' home on the Upper West Side and another in Times Square. Energized by Belmont Day, I began buying the *Daily Racing Form* on my dinner break each night on the graveyard shift and placing a bet or two at OTB the next morning before heading off on the day's assignment.

The *Form* seemed a beautiful thing, pages and pages of past performances meticulously arranged on vast broadsheet pages the same size as the *Times*. I loved that racing had its own paper, where news of wars and earthquakes was relegated to a box of brief dispatches at the bottom of page 5 while "Six to Go at Belmont" would scream across the front page. (I would later learn that the wars and earthquakes merited even a sentence only so that the *Form* could qualify for lower postal rates as a "general-interest" publication.) The *Form* cost 10 times as much as the *Times*, and since it was too expensive for a news dealer to risk theft, you had to ask for the *Form* from behind the counter, giving the simple experience of a purchase a whiff of both belonging and illicitness.

Since I was trying to build up a stake to move out, I decided to play very conservatively, looking for horses that even I, just beginning to learn about the game, could see were clearly superior and likely to win, regardless of the odds. I would bet such horses to show, I decided, and would simply make enough incredibly low-risk $100 investments to make $20 to $30 a pop.

I quickly learned, however, that trying to do this at OTB was impossible. OTB charged a 5 percent "surtax" on winning bets, meaning the payoffs were lower than they were at the track. If you bet on a 10-1 shot that paid $22 to win at Belmont, you would collect only $21 at OTB, which was keeping 5 percent of your $20 profit. At first this struck me as a fair cost for being allowed to bet conveniently—the $1 or $1.50 in profit I was giving up was still less than the cost of the round-trip train fare to Belmont and the admission fee to get into the track.

The problem was that 5 percent could actually be 50 percent, thanks to something called breakage. All payoffs at the time were rounded down to the nearest 20-cent increment so that tellers didn't have to deal with pennies and nickels. A typical show payoff on the kind of favorite I was looking for might be $2.40, but instead of taking 5 percent of the 40-cent profit on a $2 bet, which would take $2.40 to $2.38, OTB then "rounded down" $2.38 to $2.20. A $100 show bet on such a horse should have returned $120 for a $20 profit, but instead of taking my payoff down to $119, OTB took it down to $110, consuming half my profit.

My new betting scheme was out the window, but I thought I had another story. OTB was stealing money and making it impossible to win. The metro desk wasn't as excited as they had been about the pot piece, but encouraged me to go ahead and write it. I called Belmont Park for comment, and the officials there couldn't have been more helpful, telling me that this was a perfect example of why people should come out to the track instead of betting at OTB. The people at OTB insisted my story couldn't be right and besides, their customers rarely bet to show anyway.

The day before my story was scheduled to run, however, I got a call at home telling me to report to a picket line. The Newspaper Guild had joined the paper's other unions in calling a strike. No one had any idea whether it would last for days or months, but after less than two months, I was out of work.

My paycheck was gone but my days were now free to go to Belmont and get the full price on my show bets. I became a regular on the Belmont Special, the daily train that went from Penn Station to the track, and soon began joining in conversations with my fellow riders. Most of them had *Daily Racing Forms,* but the discussions usually involved their opinions about the jockeys and trainers rather than the past performances of the horses. They seemed convinced that the horses were mere tools of human intention, much of it larcenous. Perhaps because I had been introduced to racing by betting on riderless animals, it had never occurred to me to pay much attention to jockeys.

It had also never occurred to me to pay much attention to the other customers. Previously, I had considered anyone who went to the track a fellow traveler, a co-conspirator. We weren't betting against one another, we were comrades united in a quest to predict winners. Though I was skeptical of their strategy, I was just happy to be part of the unofficial fraternity on the train, and I had no glimmering that they and their opinions were in fact the basis of a winning approach to the game.

As the strike wore on and even the $50 weekly strike benefits finally ran out, I realized that I needed more of an income than my show bets were generating. I would win seven or eight of these in a row, picking up $10 or $20, but a single loser would wipe out almost all the profit.

At least I finally cashed on Alydar that summer. Racing in New York moved upstate to Saratoga for four weeks every August, and the two great rivals met for what turned out to be the last time in Saratoga's Travers Stakes. I experienced the race in the midst of the crowded 91st Street OTB parlor, where I had bet my usual $200 Alydar stake. OTB at the time was not permitted to show the races, so we all stood staring at a solid blue television screen, listening to the call of what sounded like an eventful two minutes. It was hard to tell what happened, but Alydar was blocked and stopped on the stretch turn and Affirmed might have caused the problem. Affirmed finished 1¾ lengths in front but an inquiry was posted.

After a long wait, filled with spirited debate among customers who had no idea what had happened, a disqualification was announced and the place went crazy. Half the customers were like me, thrilled to be cashing after an apparent defeat, while the others howled with outrage. One particularly fervent Affirmed fan picked up a waist-high metal trash can and heaved it across the parlor. I ducked and went to collect my $400.

The strike ended a month later. More than 100 employees had left the *Times* for good and there were plenty of job postings around the paper. The one that intrigued me was an editorial assistant's job in "op-ed," the page that ran opposite the editorial page each day and featured two opinion pieces by outside writers and two by the *Times*'s own columnists—an all-star roster that included James Reston, Tom Wicker, and my very favorite *Times* writer, Russell Baker. The other attraction would be working for Charlotte Curtis, the op-ed chief and highest-ranking woman at the paper, a viciously funny reporter who had written years of hilarious copy about high society.

I seemed completely unsuited for the job, since I had as little interest in Latin American politics or the Carter administration as I did in *Beowulf,* but when I met Charlotte I knew I wanted to work for her. She was the first person I had encountered at the *Times* who was openly and confidently critical of the paper's prissiness and pretensions. She said she wanted to lighten up the op-ed page, publish new and younger writers, and find a way to get some humor into the *Times.*

She gave me the job but cautioned me that coming to work for her could end any dreams I might have of becoming a newsroom star. The editorial and op-ed pages, operating out of offices seven floors above the newsroom, were the only parts of the paper outside Rosenthal's jurisdiction, to maintain the separation of news and opinion. A detour through the op-ed page was not part of the time-honored path from copyboy to reporter and she warned me the move might incur Rosenthal's displeasure, since his sole rival at the paper, Max Frankel, headed the editorial department.

She brightened when I told her the only job I aspired to at the *Times* was being the horse-racing writer.

"Oh, don't worry then," she said. "They couldn't care less about the sports section here. They wouldn't even have one if they didn't have to. If that's the job you want, disappear up here for a while and we'll see what we can do."

There were two obstacles to my getting the job. The first was that Steve Cady, the paper's well-liked racing writer, was only in his 40's and might well want the job for another 20 years. The second was that besides my enthusiasm, I really had no credentials or expertise beyond 18 months of amateurish gambling, most of it at greyhound tracks. Charlotte told me not to be discouraged.

"Go learn everything you can about horse racing," she said. "Become an expert. Things have a way of opening up in the newspaper business. I'll bet you a hundred bucks you'll be covering the Derby for someone inside of three years."

THE EDUCATION OF A
HORSEPLAYER

I TOOK CHARLOTTE'S ADVICE and effectively went back to college to try to become an expert. My major was horse racing rather than English literature this time around, a course of independent study with field trips to Belmont every weekend.

My instructors were the authors of everything written about the sport that I could get my hands on. I bought the *Daily Racing Form* every night, minutes after the trucks dropped off the papers at the newsstand on Broadway and 96th Street, and subscribed to all the racing magazines. I joined the Sport of Kings Society, a club of racetrack-memorabilia enthusiasts who swapped old tote tickets and racing souvenirs, and that led me to John Day, an aging book collector who sold me nearly 100 titles from his racing library for $500.

They included four massive volumes of The Jockey Club's *Racing in America* series, books I later learned traded for around $200 apiece. I ran into Day a few years later and thanked him for this treasure trove and its price. "It was worth a lot more than $500," he admitted, "but you were young so I figured, what the hell."

It was a dizzying and uneven course of study but completely consuming—a racing version of the curriculum at St. John's College in Annapolis, Maryland, where undergraduates are required to read more than 100 classics of Western civilization. Day's collection became my Great Books program, but reading them was a joy rather than an assignment. Some of the books were dense and dull and there are a few tomes on 19th-century breeding theories that have gone unread to this day, but most of the titles were captivating.

There were four main types of books: histories such as the towering Jockey Club tablets; collections by sportswriters, the best of them being Red Smith and Joe Palmer, both *Herald Tribune* alumni; reminiscences by insiders and participants; and finally, books about gambling and handicapping—mostly dreadful little get-rich-quick pamphlets, but a few of them as serious a treatment of the subject as any study of Shakespeare's imagery in his later comedies.

Tom Ainslie was the gold standard. Pictured on his dust jackets as a tidy fellow in a suit who could have passed for an accountant, Ainslie treated handicapping as neither a gambling passion nor as mathematics, but as a straightforward set of challenges to which there was a completely logical approach. Written at a time when betting horses to win was the name of the game and the most exotic wager offered anywhere was the daily double—a gimmick, to his thinking, that should be approached with caution—Ainslie advocated common sense and deductive reasoning as the tools to find the most likely winner of a race.

Ainslie's writing also struck a chord with me because of its constant undercurrent that handicapping horses was a thoroughly respectable pursuit, closer in spirit to an intense but friendly game of chess than to depraved and desperate gambling. I had by now grown accustomed to the look of faint disgust I would sometimes receive when I told people that my passion was Thoroughbred racing. It was as if I had said I were trying to break into the cock-fighting business or had developed a taste for heroin. My uncle, a professor of sociology, had greeted me at Christmas that year asking if I was "still watching stupid animals run around in circles all day."

The two other outstanding authors were Steve Davidowitz and Andrew Beyer. Davidowitz was the new generation's Ainslie, and his *Betting Thoroughbreds*, originally published in 1977, remains the first instructional book I recommend to curious newcomers to the game. Davidowitz, a minor-league pitching prospect who turned to handicapping to slake his competitive urges after blowing out his arm, updated Ainslie's work and increased its scope to consider new types of bets such as the exacta and trifecta.

Beyer was something completely different and closer to home. A Harvard undergraduate 11 years before my time, he had skipped his final exam in Chaucer to attend the 1967 Belmont Stakes and never looked back, eventually becoming the racing writer for *The Washington Post*. His first book, *Picking Winners*, detailed his early career and his development of what he called speed figures.

I skipped over the math of Beyer's figures, vaguely noting that it was something I might investigate further someday.

Besides, almost everything else I had read had advised against paying too much attention to the running times of races, which were the foundation of Beyer's figures. The quality of a horse, said most, was best measured not by the clock but by the caliber of his opposition and the stature of the races he won. Two often-repeated bromides about time were that "It's not how fast a horse runs—it's how he runs fast" and that "Time only matters when you're in jail."

Time was not a factor in the daily handicapping I was now doing while working on the op-ed page. I would leave the office for lunch each day and head straight around the corner to the OTB on Broadway. New York now had three exactas a day, on the third, fifth, and seventh races, and my standard play was to pick the race I liked best and invest $60. I would key one horse back and forth with three others in the race, a total of six bets. If I liked number 1 best and numbers 2, 4, and 6 next best, I would buy six $10 exactas: 1-2, 1-4, 1-6, and the reverse of those—the 2-1, 4-1, and 6-1. (OTB actually used letters rather than the numbers of the horses, and all bets had to be written out by hand on slips, so I would write out the combinations, such as AB or FA.)

Later in the afternoon, I would call the free results line and listen to the taped stretch call of the race and see if I had won. Only that night, when I went out to buy the next day's *Daily Racing Form,* would I have any idea how the race had been run up to the top of the stretch.

Reading handicapping books led me to other titles about other types of gambling. Horse racing, it turned out, was completely unlike gambling in a casino because your own skill could, at least in theory, make you a winner. In games such as roulette or dice, a gambler was playing against the house and the odds were tilted against him. The best a player could do was enjoy some short-term luck, but over time, defeat was a mathematical certainty.

It made absolutely no difference which numbers, colors, or rolls of the dice you bet on, because the payoff was always lower than the true chances any one of them would come up. Playing these games was as stupid as betting on the flip of a coin all day and losing more when you guessed wrong than you won when you were right. But it seemed there might be one exception.

Blackjack is a popular casino game in which the players draw cards trying to get closer to a sum of 21 than the dealer, without going over 21. The house edge comes from the fact that the players have to draw their cards first, and if they go over they lose, even if the dealer ultimately goes over 21 as well. By memorizing a set of correct decisions about when to draw more cards and when to stand, however, a player could whittle the house edge down to only about 2 percent.

In 1962, a New Mexico mathematics professor named Edward O. Thorp had written a book saying that there was a way to improve on that and actually turn the edge to the player's favor. Thorp began with the premise that if you knew which cards were coming out of the deck next, you could of course make much better decisions about when to hit and stand. The casinos obviously weren't going to deal the game face-up, but Thorp figured out that if a player could remember which cards had already been played early in the deck, he could at least know which ones were likelier to be left.

Memorizing cards sounded like something I could do, and I loved the sound of a game where the odds were in your favor. If Thorp was right—and millions of computer simulations suggested he was—the longer you played, the more you would win, and victory was as much a mathematical certainty as defeat was at the suckers' games.

So I taught myself how to "count cards." You didn't actually have to memorize each card you saw. The idea was to keep a running tally in your head of whether there had been more big (10's and picture cards) or small (3's, 4's, 5's, and 6's) cards played. If there were a lot of small cards left in the deck, that worked to the dealer's advantage, but if the unplayed cards were loaded with 10's or pictures, the player had a big edge and it was time to bet more.

In 1978, casino gambling had come to Atlantic City, New Jersey, just a two-hour bus ride from Manhattan, and once or twice a week I began making the trip after work. I would get to Resorts International about 8:00 P.M., play until the casinos were (then) required by law to close at 4:00 A.M., and arrive back in New York at dawn.

Thorp was right. If you played the correct basic strategy and varied the size of your bets depending on the "count," you had an edge that transcended winning or losing streaks. I showed a profit on 21 out of 25 trips to Atlantic City, and came to consider it a personal bank. I continued to win and moved up from the $2 to the $5 and eventually the $25 tables.

I had become a consistent winning gambler for the first time and should have been ecstatic, but within a few months I began dreading my weekly trips to the Jersey shore. The whole experience was dingy and exhausting, riding a bus in the dark and getting home at dawn with raw eyes and a splitting headache from spending eight hours chain-smoking and staring at cards.

There wasn't any sense of accomplishment in victory. Once you learned the parlor trick of counting and the rules for when to hit and stand, there were no spontaneous or creative decisions to be made at the table. Your play was completely automatic, with no opportunity to do anything clever or daring. A machine could do what I was doing. It was more like having a miserable part-time job than enjoying and winning an interesting game.

The truth was, I preferred showing a small loss handicapping a horse race and savoring its uncertainties and subtleties to grinding out a dependable profit at the casino. After a few months, I stopped visiting Atlantic City regularly and happily resumed losing on horses at OTB.

THE OP-ED JOB was a breeze. After a few months, Charlotte leapfrogged me over the other editors to be her deputy, so I had to at least pretend to take the serious stuff seriously, but we constantly conspired to subvert the page with as much offbeat and entertaining writing as possible. Charlotte let me run wild commissioning and publishing articles completely alien to the *Times*—a full page parody of *The Farmer's Almanac*, pieces about pop music and television, artwork that bordered on being an occasional comics section, and even the odd horse-racing piece.

These were the exceptions to the business of the op-ed page. The house columnists did whatever they wanted and no one changed anything but typos or spelling errors in their columns. Our job was to fill up the rest of the page with pieces from outside writers. Most of these were sober considerations of public affairs, politics, and foreign policy—not "voice of the people" opinions, but carefully crafted 800-word arguments from professors and professional residents of "think tanks," collections of academics and writers sympathetic to the political views of the tycoons who funded them.

These authors and the other op-ed editors besides Charlotte truly believed that such articles were shaping public opinion and policy and making a substantial difference in the operation of the world. Charlotte could debate welfare reform and Third World aid with the best of them but privately was cynical about the entire endeavor. To her, politics was pretty much the same as high society. People wore opinions like feathered hats and it was really all about gamesmanship and the acquisition and preservation of power.

It was almost exactly the way I had come to feel a few years earlier about literature and academia. The pinnacle of scholarship in the field I had almost followed would have been to publish a book subjecting centuries-old poetry to a new interpretation, with which the author of the previous book on the topic would probably disagree, and perhaps a professorial catfight would ensue that would boost sales from 1,000 to 1,200. It all had nothing to do with reading and enjoying books and bringing them to a wider audience.

If you were going to devote yourself to solving puzzles, the question of whether Alexander Pope had or had not been influenced by the Metaphysical poets seemed far less interesting and ultimately no more important than who was going to win the daily double at Belmont tomorrow. You could have a lot more fun and provide a lot more immediately useful information writing for racing fans than for graduate students.

LESS THAN A year into my op-ed stint, Steve Cady took early retirement. I wasn't ready for the job and didn't get it, but the next-best thing happened. The racing beat was handed to Jim Tuite, the former editor of the department, as a kind of going-away gift so he could spend a couple of years at the track before his scheduled mandatory retirement two years later. I could still gladly pay off Charlotte's $100 bet just about in time for the 1981 Derby.

Her plan was to tee me up for the job by having me become a "stringer" for the sports section, offering to fill in on Tuite's days off or travel anywhere another hand might be needed. Unfortunately, the paper gave so little space to racing that there were few such opportunities, and the department preferred to pick up an anonymous dispatch off the Associated Press wire than to pay for a proprietary story. An exception came in August of 1979, when Tuite fell ill the week of the important Alabama Stakes for 3-year-old fillies at Saratoga. The sports desk called up to the 10th floor and said that if I thought I could handle it, I could cover the Alabama.

I was going to be a racing writer, if only for a day, but it wasn't going to be easy. I had never been to Saratoga, three hours north of New York City, and still did not have a driver's license at the age of 22. I had no idea how to get there, where to stay, or how to find the track and the press box where I would be filing my story. Someone recommended taking a bus and staying at an inexpensive hotel called the Washington Inn.

I arrived at the Saratoga bus depot, the parking lot of the Spa City Diner on Broadway, the afternoon before the race wearing a blue-striped seersucker suit and carrying an electric typewriter and walked down the road to the Washington Inn, a quaint white house on a hill that offered neither food nor television. Who needed either? Saratoga seemed like the best place I had ever been—heaven, or at least summer camp, for a horseplayer, a gleaming little village where for four weeks a year everyone went to the races all day and talked about them all night. Everyone in town seemed to have a *Daily Racing Form* under his arm, and while I didn't know a soul, I felt as if they were all kindred spirits.

The 1979 Alabama was supposed to be a formality, another easy victory for Davona Dale, the nation's top 3-year-old filly. Like the now-retired Alydar, she raced for Calumet Farm, the onetime powerhouse of American racing that had produced Triple Crown winners Citation and Whirlaway but had fallen on hard times until enjoying a renaissance under a young trainer named John Veitch. Davona Dale had won the fillies' version of the Triple Crown, and the Alabama was a mere prep before she might step outside her division and take on males one week later in the Travers.

The Sunday *Times* in those days had an early Saturday deadline of 5:00 P.M., just minutes after the race would be run. My assigned 800-word story on the Alabama would consist of 750 words filed early in the day, known as B copy, and I would dictate the lead 50 words by telephone as soon as the result was official. Then I could write a fresh story all about the race and dictate that by 7:00 P.M. for the later editions of the paper that would circulate only in the city.

This system seemed somewhat dishonest. Why not just write a story about something else for the early editions and a complete story about the race for later? The answer was that the *Times* wanted its out-of-town readers to think they were getting full coverage of breaking news even if that meant tacking only one newsworthy paragraph onto a column of background material.

At least the Alabama would be an easy story for writing B copy. Davona Dale was a cinch, so 50 words about her Alabama margin of victory and time would flow nicely into a 750-word canned account of her achievements to date, which I dictated that morning from the quiet of the Washington Inn.

I lugged my typewriter to the track and eventually found the press box, a tiny wooden firetrap a rickety flight of stairs above the stands, where someone pointed me to the *Times*'s seat. I thought I recognized Beyer from his dust jacket, making a brief appearance, and throughout the afternoon I gradually matched up faces to the other bylines I had gotten to know from the New York papers and the *Form*. I was hesitant to approach anyone or to partake of what looked like a free buffet or the betting windows, and barely left my seat all day.

I eventually had to ask someone where the bathroom was. An older man in dark sunglasses and a suit pointed to a door next to his desk that bore a fresh plaque reading "The 115 Room." He explained that this summer, 115 years after its opening, Saratoga had finally put a men's room in the press box. I thanked the man, whom I had mistaken for some kind of track security chief. Only later, when I returned to my desk and picked up my *Form*, did I realize I had failed to recognize Joe Hirsch, the *Form*'s legendary columnist.

I watched the Alabama with my hand on the telephone, mentally composing clever ways to describe Davona Dale's inevitable victory. A California import named It's in the Air went to the front, and only in deep stretch did it finally dawn on me that Davona Dale wasn't going to catch her.

The next morning, *Times* readers outside the city, including those in Saratoga, read a rather curious account of the 1979 Alabama: 50 words about how It's in the Air, bearing the same flamingo-pink silks of Harbor View Farm that Affirmed had carried to the Triple Crown the previous year, had scored a historic upset victory over Davona Dale, sporting the devil's-red and blue of fabled Calumet Farm. This bulletin was followed by a 750-word tribute to the invincibility of Davona Dale, all under my byline and leading the sports section.

A few minutes after the race, I had made my way down to the winner's circle to do some reporting for my late-edition story. I asked a question of It's in the Air's trainer, Laz Barerra, whom I recognized only because he had trained Affirmed, and he responded in such a thick Cuban accent amid a noisy celebration that I could not make out a single word he said before he left. I had no idea where to find any of the jockeys or trainers in the race, and went back to the press box to dictate a story devoid of quotes.

The next morning, I cringed to see that every other writer who had covered the race had identical numerous quotes from Barrera, in flawless English. Had there been a secret press conference to which I hadn't been invited? I later learned that a track employee had gone and gotten all the quotes, typed them up, and passed them out in the press box, and that this was a standard practice in deadline sportswriting.

I felt like an idiot. I had no business covering horse racing. The only saving grace was that I still had almost two years to figure it out.

At least I didn't have to ride the bus home. My girlfriend at the time, Ruth Liebmann, was an editorial assistant at a publishing house, and her boss was a racing fan and Beyer's book editor. The editor had taken a house at Saratoga and, knowing of my interest in racing, invited Ruth to drive up from New York and for us to join them and Beyer for dinner the next night.

I might have gotten in six complete sentences during Beyer's appearance. He was glad to hear that a young horseplayer was trying to write about racing for the *Times* because "your paper's racing coverage is an absolute disgrace." I asked him what he thought of a longshot I liked the next day and he shook his head sadly and called my selection "preposterous," saying so with matter-of-fact certainty rather than rancor. (Naturally, I now had to bet twice as much as I had planned to on the horse the next day; he ran sixth.)

I had brought my copy of *Picking Winners* for Beyer to autograph at the end of the evening, but after looking at his watch frequently throughout the main course, he rose abruptly to leave before dessert, informing his dilettante dining companions that "some of us actually have work to do up here."

BACK HOME AT OTB, I was continuing my education as a horseplayer with two or three $60 exacta investments a day and I wasn't keeping track of my bets, but was surely losing. To support my betting without resuming the Atlantic City jags, I hustled up some freelance book-writing work near the bottom of the literary barrel. For $1,000, I was commissioned to turn the screenplay for *The Muppet Movie* into a novel. For the even more cringeful *The Mork and Mindy Show Scrapbook*, I recalled the site of my greyhound tripleheaders and adopted the pen name of Steven Seabrook.

I wasn't going to get much practice covering races by waiting around for people to get sick, so I began scheduling my vacations during out-of-town races and offering to cover them. Two weeks after my Alabama debacle, Spectacular Bid was making his first start since losing the Belmont and the Triple Crown with a comeback race at Delaware Park on the same day all the racing writers were covering closing day at Saratoga. This time the heavy favorite won, and by 17 lengths, but my B copy had included brief profiles of his four opponents, just in case.

In March of 1980, the desk agreed to let me cover the Santa Anita Derby, the major Kentucky Derby prep for California hopefuls. It wasn't a race the *Times* usually staffed, but since I was paying my own expenses, they agreed. At least my stuff was now considered preferable to picking up a story from the AP.

I also had figured out that what the *Times* liked even better than race coverage was an offbeat feature story, and there was a perfect one at Santa Anita that year. One of the colts on the grounds was Jaklin Klugman, who wouldn't be running in the Santa Anita Derby but was scheduled to come east for the Kentucky Derby. His owner, the actor and *Odd Couple* star Jack Klugman, was a huge racing fan and visited his colt most mornings. Klugman agreed to a long interview and the *Times* gave the story a splashy play.

In the Santa Anita Derby, Raise a Man was the 3-5 favorite but he came up empty and the winner was Codex, a 25-1 shot trained by D. Wayne Lukas, a recent convert from Quarter Horse racing. Fortunately, because of the time difference between New York and California, there was no way to get a quick result into the first edition. Had there been, I surely would have told *Times* readers that a new contender for the Kentucky Derby had emerged that afternoon. About 15 minutes after the race, Lukas came up to the press box to be interviewed and had to explain that Codex was such a surprising late bloomer that no one had nominated him to the Derby before the deadline and now it was too late.

Lukas, who would go on to revolutionize training over the next two decades and win four Derbies, never again failed to nominate all the 3-year-olds in his barn. Nor did I ever cover a Derby prep again without a list of Triple Crown nominees in my briefcase.

I had been impressed with Codex's victory. I was beginning to trust my own visual observations of races, and it seemed to me that Codex had done some special things that were the mark of a seriously good horse. He had made three different moves during the race, battled Raise a Man into defeat, and still held off a strong late charge from Rumbo. The two of them were almost eight lengths clear of the rest. Two weeks later in the Hollywood Derby, they met again and this time Codex had a cleaner trip and beat Rumbo by two lengths.

Since Codex would not be permitted to run in the Kentucky Derby, I backed the next best thing in Rumbo. The two favorites for the 1980 Derby, Rockhill Native and Plugged Nickle, were both front-runners, and if they hooked up and knocked each other out early, I thought Rumbo would benefit and could blow by the field in the stretch. The theory worked out to near perfection, but a horse I had never considered—a filly named Genuine Risk—got an even better trip behind the duel and held off Rumbo and Jaklin Klugman to win by a length.

No filly had won the Derby since Regret in 1915, not that very many had tried. Why run a filly against colts when fillies had their own rich races? Genuine Risk's owners, Bert and Diana Firestone, thought it was worth a shot and everything worked out perfectly for her. The result was hailed as a triumph for women's liberation and got much more attention nationally than the victories of the three great previous Derby winners—Seattle Slew, Affirmed, and Spectacular Bid.

I found it all exasperating. General sports columnists and television commentators who knew little about racing and watched exactly three races a year were hailing Genuine Risk as a wonder horse, clearly the best filly in 65 years. The "girl" had beaten the "boys," which might be a cute story, but to my mind did not necessarily mean that Genuine Risk was a great horse—especially since the horse I thought was the best of the males had not been allowed to run in the Derby.

I couldn't wait to bet Codex against her in the Preakness. Handicappers looking only at the raw past-performance lines would see that Codex had beaten Rumbo once by a neck and once by two lengths, whereas Genuine Risk had beaten him by a length, and conclude that Genuine Risk and Codex were roughly equal in ability. I felt that I knew better.

It was the first time I had a passionate handicapping opinion in a Triple Crown race. I had gone down cheering three times with Alydar, but out of loyalty and affection, not because I could make a compelling and logical case that he was the better horse and deserved to win. I told everyone I knew to back Codex and pulled together $500 to bet him at OTB. I went back to my apartment and watched with glee as Codex blew past Genuine Risk on the turn, brushing her slightly as he barreled away and won by 4¾ lengths.

Genuine Risk's rider claimed foul, but the stewards disallowed the objection and Codex paid $7.40 as the third choice. I collected over $1,800 and felt smart and vindicated, but in the days ahead was made to feel that I had profited from a heinous offense. The sportswriters of America decided as one that Genuine Risk was a sweet old lady whose purse had been stolen by a knife-wielding assailant. "Filly Mugged!" was the headline in more than one paper. Even the *Daily Racing Form,* which rarely printed editorials or opinion pieces of any kind, ran a front-page screed entitled "Rodeo Cordero" accusing Codex's jockey, Angel Cordero Jr., of rough riding against the poor little filly and crimes against humanity in general.

I found the entire issue absurd. Had Codex won by a neck, perhaps the faint brushing between the two horses could be considered relevant, but he had won by nearly five widening lengths. Genuine Risk had not come after him or gained ground after the incident, instead falling back farther with each stride behind a faster horse. The filly's advocates argued she had been intimidated and had "lost momentum," phrases that appeared in the *Form's* unusually descriptive chart footnotes for the race.

The Firestones appealed the stewards' decision to the Maryland Racing Commission, which after a three-day media circus of hearings rightly decided to leave the result alone.

It set up an intriguing Belmont rematch, but the showdown fizzled on a muddy track. Codex was through after a mile and came out of the race with a career-ending injury. At least a 53-1 shot, Temperence Hill, came lumbering up late to catch Genuine Risk. If he hadn't, people would believe to this day that she was unfairly deprived of a Triple Crown.

I WAS BEGINNING to visit racetracks like a collector, savoring each new acquisition and always making sure to get a T shirt, ashtray, or some tote tickets. That winter I had gone to Florida for the first time and driven around the state, adding three Thoroughbred, two harness, and seven greyhound tracks to my portfolio.

I pitched a book cataloguing all these visits to a publisher named Workman, which a few months earlier had offered me a comedy project called *The Preppie Handbook*. I had turned it down, and it went on to sell a zillion copies. Instead, I got a $5,000 advance for the racetrack book. Another publisher, which had brought out *The Harvard Lampoon Big Book of College Life,* signed me to do a collection of short stories and humor pieces. I had never written a word of fiction, but it was another $5,000, and I had begun to crave something that cost exactly that much.

The advance equaled the price tag for a trip I had seen advertised in the *Form*: Mike Warren's Red Carpet Racing Tour, a 10-day jaunt to England and France culminating in the Prix de l'Arc de Triomphe at Longchamp in Paris, the continent's premier fall race. Warren, whose primary business was selling his "professional" tips on horses and football games to mailing lists of gamblers, seemed to be trying to rehabilitate his image as a shady tout and position himself as a champagne-sipping jet-setter.

I wrote away for the brochure, which promised a luxury tour surrounded by famous racing personalities and surefire tips on the European races. I had been to England and Ireland once before, living out of a backpack and staying in youth hostels to visit the graves of great poets at Westminster Abbey and retrace Leopold Bloom's steps through the streets of Dublin from James Joyce's *Ulysses*. I loved the idea of going back to Europe, traveling in style and visiting racetracks instead of literary landmarks,

Spending $5,000 on a 10-day trip seemed slightly insane, since $5,000 was approximately 100 percent of my net worth, but I had begun to develop the sometimes healthy and sometimes clearly irresponsible lack of respect for money common to frequent bettors. My weekly paycheck was $250 after taxes, but I was pushing at least twice that much through the OTB windows every week, and the routine swing of a photo finish could mean a difference of a month's pay. So $5,000 for the trip of a lifetime seemed almost reasonable. Besides, what better way for me to lend an international dimension to the racetracks book, add some exotic new tracks to my collection, and perhaps meet some of the people I hoped to be covering by the next Derby?

So off I went. It hadn't occurred to me that a 23-year-old bachelor might not be the typical demographic on this trip, and I found myself the odd man out among 20 older couples. The only racing celebrity turned out to be the *Daily Racing Form*'s cartoonist, Pierre Bellocq, better known as Peb, who did a brisk business sketching the members of our tour group and selling them their caricatures. Peb turned out to be a great travel companion, full of stories about the track and his native France.

It was a grand tour of places I had only read about—the racecourses at Epsom and Ascot, the National Stud at Newmarket, the training center overlooked by ancient castles at Chantilly. These were the sites I wanted to correlate to my reading the same way I had with Shakespeare's grave or Joyce's house six years earlier.

The glimpses I got of racing in England and France were mostly baffling. A day at the races was a far more festive occasion than it was back home. The tracks were filled with champagne stands and oyster bars and people seemed to be having animated discussions of the upcoming race instead of studying their past performances in solitude. In part this was because there were no past performances. *The Sporting Life,* Britain's version of the *Form,* instead offered a largely textual description of each horse's recent races, and the players considered written reports of how well the horses had been training more important than any statistical analysis.

This reflected an entirely different style of racing. All the races were run on grass, and for most of the way, the horses appeared to be under restraint and just galloping along. Turning for home, everyone was let loose and there would be a mad dash to the wire. Early pace and position, huge factors in American dirt racing, were nearly irrelevant. I had no idea what I was looking at or how anyone could bet on this stuff, but I did manage to recoup a quarter of the cost of the trip by betting on the Arc winner. My highly scientific method was to choose the horse with the most American name: The French insisted on calling her "Duh-twah," but I was betting on a filly named Detroit.

The other lasting friendship I made on the tour besides Peb's was with Leo Veitch and his new bride, Lynne. Leo was a horse trainer, the brother of Hall of Famer Syl Veitch and the uncle of John Veitch of Calumet and Alydar fame. Lynne was an exercise rider and a jazz singer, and once we established my piano-playing past we were inseparable throughout the trip. Every night we ended up in a different pub or bistro where Leo told me racing stories, drank me under the table, and then demanded that Lynne and I take over the piano.

The friendship continued when we got back home. I finally had a friend on the inside of the game whose stable I could stop by at Belmont Park and who would answer any question I had about how racing really worked. Leo and Lynne began inviting me to highly liquid dinner parties on Long Island, where I got to know the rest of the Veitch clan and where the guest list might also include family friends such as the trainer Elliott Burch and the jockey Eddie Maple.

I came away from those dinners increasingly aware of a huge gap between horseplayers and the participants. These trainers and jockeys had among them won most of the nation's great races with numerous champions, and I greedily pumped them for their stories, but none of them approached racing the way that I or any bettor did.

They had little interest in the intricacies of handicapping and betting. The customers were sort of a necessary evil, disrespectful loudmouths whose opinions were worthless because they didn't know the first thing about galloping a horse or bandaging his legs. These horsemen, as they liked to be called, were totally focused on their own runners and whether they were eating and training well, regardless of the type of race or competition they would be facing.

They truly loved a "good" horse, as giddy an adjective as

they would ever use for even a Hall of Famer, and were almost religiously respectful of those runners who had proved their quality. Yet they were utterly without sentiment for the majority of the breed. I listened in horror one night as an elderly trainer wistfully recalled a bygone era when he would go to a Kentucky farm each year to inspect his owner's new crop of 2-year-olds.

"You put the good ones on a van to New York and you put the others out back in a ditch and shot them," he recalled. There seemed to be general agreement that those were indeed the good old days.

THE PUBLISHER WHO had signed up the racetrack book lost interest and I never had to deliver a manuscript, but there was no getting out of the book of light fiction. I holed up and in two months batted out a collection called *Offtrack*, whose two longest stories were an account of betting on Rooster Cogburn and Downing at Wonderland and the slightly fictional tale of an English major who preferred going to OTB. The book got a handful of complimentary reviews but sold about as many copies as my thesis on the Metaphysical poets would have.

Still, I figured having a racing-themed book to my name would only help get the *Times* job, but as 1981 began there was no movement despite a new and well-placed ally. The *Times* had recruited an editor from *Sports Illustrated*, Sandy Padwe, to be the deputy editor of the sports department. On Padwe's second day of work, he was asked to pick a six-letter password for the *Times's* new computer system and he typed in the name of his favorite racehorse: A-l-y-d-a-r. The system told him that another employee had already chosen that password and he demanded to know who at *The New York Times* could possibly have made such a choice. That led him to me, and he began pressing to move me off the op-ed page and onto the racing beat.

Despite his efforts and Charlotte Curtis's, though, nothing was happening. Tuite's retirement date was June 1, and the idea had been for me to start full-time in April to allow a transition. As the 1981 Derby approached, all the paperwork had been filled out for me to move to the sports department, but it seemed to have gone into a black hole. Finally, Charlotte went directly to Abe Rosenthal and asked what the problem was. It turned out he was personally offended that I had never come to him to discuss my career choice. He was sitting on the paperwork until I did.

So I went to him, apologized profusely, and sought his blessing. He gave it conditionally: He would be very disappointed if I didn't get bored with racing within three years and come back to his newsroom. At 24, he said, I was still young enough to become a metro reporter at 27 and move on to Washington or Prague and eventually back to the newsroom as an editor. Racing could be a great beat for a young writer, he allowed, but it was a terrible world because of the gambling—he knew because his father had been involved with bookmakers. If I stayed around the track for more than three years, he said, it meant I was a gambler and not a writer.

I nodded and said that I wasn't committed to a life in racing, crossing my fingers as I lied.

GETTING UP TO SPEED

So I was the racing writer for *The New York Times*—almost. It was too close to the Derby to switch horse reporters in midstream, and Tuite wanted to cover one more Triple Crown. The sports department told me to go anyway for the experience, so I spent my first Derby and Preakness as a kind of shadow reporter, writing feature stories and sidebars and staying out of Tuite's way.

It was another one of those years when the fastest 3-year-olds were highly suspect sprinters who would fail to negotiate the classic distances. Pleasant Colony, a late-blooming stretch-runner, emerged from obscurity in one of the final Derby preps, overtaking heavily favored Cure the Blues to win

Aqueduct's Wood Memorial with a powerful rush that made him look like he could handle 1¼ miles in the Derby.

Johnny Campo, his trainer, had been a successful fixture on the New York scene but had never had a horse this good or a national stage, and he was determined to enjoy it. A short, round man with a gravelly voice and hostile demeanor, Campo spent Derby Week saying his colt was a cinch, the competition was a bunch of "rats," and that he had forgotten more about horses than the rest of the Derby trainers knew.

When Pleasant Colony won the Derby, most of the coverage of the race told the story of an unlikely triumph by a buffoonish and loudmouthed New Yorker. Instead of feeling vindicated, Campo thought he was being mocked as a minor character out of *Guys and Dolls* rather than being given his due as a world-class horse trainer.

I was entirely sympathetic. I had spent my first Derby Week lurking at the back of the pack of sportswriters that roamed from one Derby trainer to another in the mornings leading up to the race. These days are the least newsworthy of the entire Derby season; the horses have run their preps, their final training consists of fairly routine and uninformative workouts to keep them on edge, and everyone is just waiting around for the race to be run. Unfortunately, newspapers and television stations give more coverage to racing during this brief window than in practically the rest of the year combined, so journalists have to generate hefty stories from slim news.

Derby Week had been my first exposure to this process and to the nation's traveling core of big-name general sports columnists, who were usually attending their only race of the year. The generalists covered a different major event in some other sport every week and stood around Churchill Downs together in the mornings, swapping tales of the Super Bowl and Wimbledon and complaining about the hotel rooms in Louisville or the poor selection of press-room pastries compared to those at the Masters.

These writers knew enough about the mainstream sports not to embarrass themselves, but when it came to racing, they lacked the background and expertise to know what they were looking at. Instead of writing about how a race shaped up or reporting on any late developments, they searched for "colorful" personalities and details and wove them into what editors admiringly call human-interest stories. If a longshot's jockey had a sick grandmother, that was their column. A Johnny Campo was an even rarer gift.

The morning after Pleasant Colony won the Preakness with ease, Campo held court outside the colt's stall. His chief interrogator was an ancient and popular sports columnist for New York's *Daily News,* whose main beat was baseball. Campo was guaranteeing a Belmont victory and a Triple Crown for his colt, not only because of his superior trainer but also because Campo thought he was still improving and maturing.

"He was a late foal, a May foal," Campo said. "He may not even be three years old yet."

Everyone who thought about racing more than three times a year knew exactly what Campo meant. All racehorses are deemed to have a common birthday, and every 2-year-old officially becomes a 3-year-old on January 1 even though he might have been foaled anywhere from January to June. The *Daily Racing Form* did not publish actual foaling dates at the time, and Campo had revealed a new and interesting piece of information about the colt.

The *News* columnist, however, had discovered the crime of the century.

"You mean, you're only telling us now," he sputtered, "after he wins the Derby and the Preakness, that this horse wasn't even eligible for those races?"

The rest of the regular racing press let out a collective groan and a few people tried to nudge the columnist and tell him he was barking up the wrong tree, but he continued to insist that Campo had been running some sort of a scam. Campo stormed off muttering about "these morons," and I couldn't blame him.

Pleasant Colony ran third behind Summing and Highland Blade in the Belmont and the world stopped paying attention to Campo. About a week later, now officially the *Times*'s racing writer, I went by Campo's barn at Belmont to see what the summer plans were for the horse. I introduced myself as the new guy and Campo wasn't shy about welcoming me to the job.

"Let me tell you something, and learn to listen carefully when the Fat Man tells you something," he began. "You don't know nothing. Nothing. Whatever you think you know, you don't know it. You want to learn about this game, you stay close to the Fat Man and maybe you'll learn something.

"And another thing," he said. "I don't know you from something I'd scrape off my shoe but I seen you around with the other reporters. I seen you wearing a trench coat. Only one guy in the press box gets to wear a trench coat and that's Mr. Joe Hirsch who's the only guy up there who's got a clue. Don't let me see you back here in a trench coat again and maybe you'll be okay."

Campo's opinion of Hirsch was universal around the racetrack. Hirsch was the hardest-working turf writer in the country, combing the stables every morning for news. He considered himself not only a pipeline for official news through the *Form*, but also an ambassador for the sport, presenting it in its most favorable light while always comporting himself as a gentleman and diplomat. He had no interest in turning over rocks to look for trouble, nor did he feel it was part of his job. He believed certain things were best left unsaid and most problems should be solved quietly behind closed doors.

His work ethic was unbelievable. Every spring he single-handedly covered the run-up to the Triple Crown with an exhaustive daily report, "Derby Doings," which might list as many as 30 horses being considered for the race. Joe hunted down every one of them each day. Racetrack officials and reporters from around the country called Joe to find out who was pointing for the Derby, not the other way around. *Form* readers looked forward to the annual debut of "Derby Doings" as a more reliable confirmation of springtime than the first robin.

Part of Joe's ambassadorial role was to nurture new additions to the press box, to help them track down people and stories so that racing would get as much space as possible in the sports pages of daily general newspapers. Joe was so wide-ly recognized as a steady mentor for young people that Sonny Werblin, who owned a string of racehorses as well as the New York Jets, turned to Hirsch in 1965 to provide guidance and stability to a newcomer to New York: Joe Namath, whom Werblin moved into Hirsch's Manhattan apartment.

When I officially got the *Times* job, I became Joe's new project. The amount of coverage *The New York Times* gave racing was particularly important to the sport, and it was both Joe's self-appointed duty and his natural kindness to younger writers that made him my guardian. He would occasionally share breaking news with me because he felt it was more important for the *Times* to report something than for him to have an exclusive in the *Form*. He would sometimes ask me to join him on morning rounds at the track or for dinner in

Manhattan after the races, and he would not hear of splitting a check, much less surrendering one entirely.

One time after Joe had again picked up the tab for an extravagant meal, I asked him if there wasn't something I could do for him in return.

"Always wear a necktie when you go to the paddock," was his lone request, and I honored it for nearly a decade.

ONE OF THE best parts of the new job was that I would be going to Saratoga for the whole meeting, and could pick out a small house at the *Times*'s expense. The entire Belmont community would pack up and head to the Adirondacks for the four weeks of Saratoga, moving into rented houses and apartments.

The highlight of my first full Saratoga season was spending a week sitting next to Red Smith, who was in his final year as a *Times* columnist. Unlike the other generalists, Smith knew and genuinely liked racing. He spent a week at Saratoga each year, not to weigh in on the Travers like the other visiting sportswriters, but to enjoy the town and the people around the track.

"There are more stories per square foot at the racetrack than anywhere else in sports," he said. "If there are eighty horses running today, there are at least eighty stories, all of them more interesting than who won or lost a ballgame."

Smith found my unorthodox route to the racetrack amusing, and he encouraged me to "keep doing what you love" and not to let the *Times* turn me into a baseball or political writer. My proudest professional moment of the year was when, before filing his column that week, he asked me to "look it over and see if I got anything wrong."

Pleasant Colony returned to racing in the Travers, losing by a head to the mud-loving longshot Willow Hour over a sloppy

Saratoga track, and three weeks later beat older horses to win the Woodward Stakes back at Belmont. Then in the Marlboro Cup, he ran a thoroughly flat race finishing a bad fourth, completely failing to fire. Such a performance is often a sign of injury, but Campo assured me the horse was fine and would prove his greatness by coming back in the Jockey Club Gold Cup, where a victory could still make him the Horse of the Year.

A few days before that race, I happened to be spending the morning around the Belmont stables, interviewing the trainers of Gold Cup horses. I went by Campo's barn a few times but missed him. I asked a couple of the grooms or assistants if Pleasant Colony had been to the track or was going to work out that day and was told that the colt had not left his stall all morning.

I went up to the press box and a publicity-department aide handed me a news release hot off the copying machine: It said that Pleasant Colony had suffered a freak accident while breaking from the starting gate in a workout that morning and was being retired. I phoned the track clockers, who surely would have witnessed such an incident—this was the Derby, Preakness, and Woodward winner.

The clockers told me they would bet their lives that the horse had not been to the track, much less suffered a starting-gate accident, that morning. They hadn't seen the press release. An hour later one of them called back and begged me not to quote them by name. "We've been told that's the story," he said. I tried without success to find Campo, right up until deadline.

I reported the whole story, quoting the clockers anonymously. The next day, the *Times*'s sports editor, Joe Vecchione, called and told me in an amused voice that he had received two phone calls from men identifying themselves only as friends of Campo's and saying that I was an anti-Italian liar who, along with the *Times,* would pay for what had been in the paper. Vecchione said he had politely dismissed the callers and told me to keep up the good work.

Unsigned mail continued to arrive for weeks, and Campo never talked to me again. One of his sons saw me in the paddock a few weeks later and unleashed an enormous gob of spit onto my shoes. Two years later, Eddie Maple unwittingly invited me and Campo to the same small dinner party. I sat down on a lawn chair to Campo's left and he got up, picked up his chair, and turned it so his back was to me and refused to make eye contact during an uncomfortable evening for all.

The fundamentals of Pleasant Colony's peculiar retirement, if not the theatrics, would play themselves out again and again as I covered the sport over the next few years. Racehorses were becoming bigger business than ever, and preserving their reputations sometimes meant being less than forthright with the press.

Thoroughbreds are poorly constructed creatures, half a ton of speed crashing down repeatedly on spindly legs, and it is the exception when one stays sounds for his entire career. Pleasant Colony could have gone wrong at practically any time that fall, but Campo, and the breeders who were buying pieces of the colt for future stud duty, felt it would somehow damage his value to say that he had simply become unsound, the way most racehorses eventually do. It was somehow preferable to concoct a completely unforeseen occurrence such as a starting-gate mishap than to admit a horse was sore or sour.

Everyone in racing had been spoiled in the 1970's by a succession of amazingly fast, durable superstars. Six out of 10 champion 2-year-olds had returned to win the Kentucky Derby the next year. There had been three Triple Crown winners, and the decade had ended with three horses who were champions at 2, 3, and 4 in Seattle Slew, Affirmed, and Spectacular Bid. In the intervening years, not a single horse has achieved any of those feats.

The decade of greatness had sparked a renaissance of high-stakes interest in the sport, and Thoroughbred bloodstock was about to become a precious commodity for speculation. Foreign investors, and Americans seeking to take advantage of newly legislated tax shelters that made owning and breeding an attractive financial dodge, were starting to bid up both unraced yearlings and stallion prospects to dizzying and unsustainable heights.

That summer, I had attended the inaugural running of the world's first million-dollar race, the Arlington Million at Arlington Park outside Chicago, where the 6-year-old gelding John Henry scored a desperate victory and went on to beat Pleasant Colony in the voting for Horse of the Year. John Henry would again win that race and that title three years later as a 9-year-old folk hero. The only reason he was still running was that he was a gelding, useless to the breeders.

Despite million-dollar prizes, the big money now was in a horse's perceived value at stud, not in the sum of the purses he could win in even the biggest races. Affirmed's owners said they had actually lost money racing him as a 4-year-old despite winning six of the sport's 10 richest races because the insurance premiums alone outweighed the purses.

Secretariat, the greatest champion of the 1970's and perhaps of any decade, had been syndicated for $6 million in 1973. Now Pleasant Colony, far less accomplished and as physically unattractive a Derby winner as anyone could recall, was worth $12 million. The market, however, would soar three times higher than that peak over the next two years for a pair of colts who would introduce me to an entirely new way of looking at racing.

THE 1982 TRIPLE CROWN season would be the first I would cover in its entirety, and to stay on top of it I began a clerical task I have maintained ever since. Nowadays I use a computer spreadsheet for my "Derby book," but for the first 10 years I bought an 80-page spiral-bound notebook of graph paper and devoted a two-page spread to each of the major prep races leading up to the Derby.

On the left-hand page, I would paste in the nominations for each race, which were usually published two or three weeks in advance. On the right-hand side, I would paste in the *Daily Racing Form*'s chart of the race, and below it in my neatest handwriting were columns of figures "breaking down" the race—a calculation of each runner's actual fractional times.

Especially after seeing favored front-runners collapse in the 1980 and 1981 Derbies, I had become convinced that the key to the race was finding the best finisher, a horse that would still be running well at the end while the others were struggling. This might seem like an easy task that could be accomplished with a quick look at the past performances to see who had been gaining ground at the end of shorter races.

I had come to realize, however, that my beloved running lines could be misleading. A horse whose past-performance line might make it look as if he had been closing like a hurricane at the end of the race might just have been clunking up late while the dueling pacesetters staggered home in glacial time. Only by calculating each horse's actual finishing time, I had decided, could I know which horses had the most potential to stretch out successfully on Derby Day.

As I began to break down races this way, not just the 1982 preps but previous years' Derbies as well, I was stunned to see for the first time that much of racing was an optical illusion. From the way most races looked—front-runners sprinting to the lead and trying to hold on while stretch-runners lingered early and made gallant late charges—I had assumed that half the horses were running faster early and the other half were running their fastest at the end.

In the unforgiving light of actual running times, I saw this was not the case. The front-runners indeed were slowing down with each passing quarter-mile, but so were most of the apparent stretch-runners. They were usually decelerating too, just less drastically than the speed horses.

Horses are not timed individually in races. Only the leader's time is recorded at each point of call, and you have to extrapolate every other horse's actual time by seeing how far behind the leader he is at that stage of the race. At the time I used the handy assumption—common around the racetrack, but ultimately wrong—that a length is equal to a fifth of a second. (It's actually closer to a sixth.)

Here is a simplistic illustration. In a one-mile race, suppose that a front-runner leads from start to finish and runs the mile in one minute and 39 seconds (1:39). His times, posted after each quarter-mile, might be :23, :47, 1:12, and 1:39. From this we can extrapolate that his four quarter-miles were run in 23, then 24 (the difference between 23 and 47), then 25, and finally 27 seconds.

Let's say that another horse in this race is five lengths behind the leader at each of the first three calls, then appears to mount a tremendous late rally and finishes on nearly even terms with the leader, losing a photo-finish by a nose. His past-performance line will show him advancing through the field while remaining five lengths behind the leader and then making up all but a nose of it with a rush. Their running lines might look like this:

Leader	1-5	1-5	1-5	1-nose
"Closer"	4-5	3-5	2-5	2-nose

The runner-up looks like a hero, finishing furiously to erase all but an inch from a five-length disadvantage. But if we compare their actual quarter-mile times, a lot of the gallantry disappears from the runner-up's near miss:

Leader	23	24	25	27
"Closer"	24	24	25	26

Both horses are tiring, one worse than the other because he exerted himself early. Yet to this day, most horseplayers who see a race like this will bet the runner-up next time because he "finished well" and "just missed." Most sportswriters would describe such a contest in epic terms, with the game and gritty leader "digging down" and "finding a second gear" to hold off the noble closer who was "flying" at the end.

I was hunting for Derby candidates who were truly finishing well, not just looking that way in the running lines, but I was having trouble finding one in the preps of 1982 until I worked on the chart of the March 21 San Felipe Handicap. The race was at a mile and a sixteenth, and I broke it into its first four quarter-miles and then the final sixteenth of a mile.

I was less interested in the winner, the flashy front-runner Advance Man, than in the runner-up. My notebook, where I expressed fifths of a second as decimals (so 23.2 meant $23\frac{2}{5}$) looked like this:

Advance Man	23.2	24.0	24.1	24.3	6.0
Gato Del Sol	25.2	23.2	23.4	24.1	5.2

Advance Man had won by a neck as the favorite but had been slowing down during every quarter in the race. Gato Del Sol, however, accelerated in his middle quarters, ran a solid fourth quarter, then truly zoomed home in the final sixteenth.

Two weeks later a colt named Muttering won the Santa Anita Derby and Gato Del Sol ran what looked like a dull fourth. I was disappointed that Gato Del Sol had not improved stretching out a bit longer from $1\frac{1}{16}$ to $1\frac{1}{8}$ miles, but was encouraged by his final furlong (eighth of a mile):

Muttering	23.1	23.0	24.1	24.4	12.3
Gato Del Sol	25.0	23.0	23.2	25.0	11.4

I was further consoled that there seemed to be a reason for his regression to a slow fourth quarter before his final burst: According to the chart, he had "swung out very wide rallying into the stretch."

Gato Del Sol had his final prep in Keeneland's Blue Grass Stakes against heavily favored Linkage, a quick pace-presser who had won a sprint over the track a week earlier. I bet Gato Del Sol enthusiastically and watched in disbelief as Linkage grabbed the lead after a quarter-mile and widened his margin to win by $5\frac{1}{2}$ lengths, with Gato Del Sol barely getting up for second. The breakdown didn't make it look any better:

Linkage	23.4	22.4	23.2	25.1	12.4
Gato Del Sol	24.2	23.2	23.2	24.4	13.0

I was through with Gato Del Sol. Asked to keep contact

with the field and run a little faster earlier, he had come up empty late. He had actually finished with a slower final furlong than a horse that had run much faster earlier in the race. I would find my Derby winner elsewhere.

The prep breakdown that now intrigued me most was Aqueduct's Wood Memorial, where the first three finishers' fractions looked like this:

Air Forbes Won	24.2	23.1	24.1	25.4	13.2
Shimatoree	23.4	23.3	24.0	26.0	13.3
Laser Light	26.2	22.4	23.2	25.2	13.2

Laser Light's final furlong was nothing special and a couple of stragglers in the field had come closer to 13 flat over the dull Aqueduct track. But after his extremely slow first quarter, Laser Light had run the fastest second, third, and fourth quarters of anyone in the 10-horse field. I had never seen that before in a chart breakdown. I had my Derby horse, and he was 18-1 when the gates opened.

It was another Derby where the favorites, Air Forbes Won and El Baba, pressed a quick pace and folded. I was not exactly thrilled when Gato Del Sol got the jump on Laser Light from the back of the pack and ran the race I'd expected before his lackluster Blue Grass. He took the lead with a furlong to go and drew off by 2½ lengths, paying $44.40 to win, as Laser Light moved belatedly to get up for second. Gato Del Sol had scored the biggest Derby upset in 15 years, and I had learned a valuable lesson about deserting a 21-1 shot off one disappointing race.

It was to be a Triple Crown season unlike any before or since, due to three highly unconventional decisions by the trainers of three horses. The first had been Henry Clark's choice to skip the Kentucky Derby with Linkage, who would have been the heavy favorite off his Blue Grass and whose absence seemed all the stranger after Gato Del Sol came back to win the roses. Clark, an elderly Marylander with more interest in winning his home state's Preakness, simply thought Linkage needed a breather after racing twice at Keeneland in April.

Clark was widely praised for resisting temptation and putting his horse's well-being first, but when Gato Del Sol's trainer did the same he became a pariah. Eddie Gregson, a thoughtful young Californian, announced after the Derby that he was skipping the Preakness because the colt was unlikely to thrive at the shorter distance and would benefit from a five-week break before the Belmont.

It was heresy to forego a chance at the Triple Crown. Without the Derby winner in the field, the Preakness held little national interest, and Pimlico management turned its frustration on Gregson. Chick Lang, the track's proud and pugnacious general manager, arranged for a goat to be placed in the stall traditionally reserved for the Derby winner and publicly questioned Gregson's sanity and masculinity.

The circus feel of that Preakness Week was amplified by the presence of Cupecoy's Joy, a filly who had been a surprise entrant in the Derby and had gunned to the lead, helping to doom the favorites' chances by forcing them to chase fast fractions, before tiring to finish 10th. When she arrived at Pimlico, everyone assumed that the experiment of running her against colts was over and that she was there for the shorter and easier Black Eyed Susan Stakes for fillies rather than the Preakness a day later.

Her owner, Robert Perez, showed up at Pimlico bleary-eyed and more than a little grumpy after a drive from New York that had detoured through a long and expensive evening at Atlantic City's casinos. When he got there and found that his beloved filly had been housed in one of the stalls reserved for Black Eyed Susan entrants instead of with the colts pointing for the Preakness, he pitched a fit and took her back to New York.

I had my own blowup that week, my first tiff with the *Daily Racing Form*. When I had broken down the Derby chart, the final fractions for several horses simply didn't make sense or jibe with my memory of how the race had been run. I had watched Laser Light closely as he made a wide rush before simply being outrun in the stretch by a drawing-away Gato Del Sol, but according to the chart, he had been ninth with a furlong to go and had run the race's fastest final quarter. I knew he had been closer and had not finished all that strongly.

I wrote a small item in the *Times* early in Preakness Week questioning the accuracy of the Derby chart, arrived in Baltimore the next night, and saw Joe Hirsch sitting in the hotel bar. I rushed over to greet my mentor, but he stared straight ahead when I sat down next to him. I asked him if he was okay.

"No, I'm not," he said. "I feel like someone plunged a cold knife into my back. That was a terrible thing you wrote in the *Times*, terrible for racing and for the *Form*."

He turned away, my company clearly unwelcome. I was personally devastated by his rejection but also self-righteously indignant. It wasn't my job to promote the *Form*'s infallibility. I had actually believed the *Form* would be willing to correct the historical record. Still, I was greatly relieved a few days later when Joe greeted me as if nothing had happened. Our friendship resumed and we never spoke of the incident again.

It turned out that Robert Perez's Atlantic City detour and subsequent tantrum over stall assignments may well have decided the 1982 Preakness. Linkage was the odds-on favorite in a field of just seven that now included only one front-runner, a stretching-out miler named Aloma's Ruler, who waltzed to the lead and slowed down the pace—a first half-mile in a dawdling 48 seconds, as opposed to the 46⅕ Cupecoy's Joy had posted in the Derby. The legendary Bill Shoemaker on Linkage waited and waited behind the slow fractions and then fell short of catching the leader by half a length at the wire.

The Belmont loomed as a rubber match to settle the 3-year-old title among Gato Del Sol, who had skipped the Preakness, and Linkage and Aloma's Ruler, who had passed the Derby. A three-way showdown seemed like the story five days before the race, a Monday afternoon when the traditional Memorial Day feature at Belmont Park was the Metropolitan Handicap.

The Met, run at a mile around one turn over Belmont's sweeping track, was the most prestigious race of the year for milers. I had read about the exploits of old-time trainers who had used the Met as a springboard to the Belmont, but that was in an earlier era when horses were sturdier and might run twice in the same week. Now it was primarily a race for the top older horses and for sprinting 3-year-olds who had been held out of the Triple Crown because of distance limitations.

The Met favorite seemed to be one of those 3-year-olds. Conquistador Cielo had won the Saratoga Special as a 2-year-old but was sidelined from August to February with injuries and then went on the shelf again after running in two Florida sprints. He had returned to win two races, including an 11-length romp at a mile.

He rocketed out of the gate in the Met but had company vying for the lead, and it would have been understandable had he wilted after winning the early duel. Instead, after six furlongs in 1:09, he drew away with a strong fourth quarter in 24 seconds to win by 7¼ lengths, stopping the timer in 1:33 flat to set a track record.

It was an amazing performance, rivaled only by what his trainer said after the race, an idea so outlandish I almost didn't report it until I confirmed that I had heard him correctly: Woody Stephens said he was thinking of running the colt back in the Belmont Stakes five days later.

Woody was the king of New York's trainers, the only one who merited two barns on the Belmont backstretch, and those stalls were filled with some of the nation's best-bred horses. He had won almost every important race at some point during his 50 years around the track, with runners of all types and ages, but his specialty was younger horses. His 2-year-olds fired early and often. He had won the 100th Kentucky Derby with Cannonade in 1974, and with one of those trophies under his belt, he seemed less obsessed about that race than many trainers.

He knew there were plenty of other prizes worth winning and he believed in letting a horse drag him to a race and not the reverse. He would back off a horse if he felt he was asking too much, but conversely was aggressive about what he called "making some hay while the sun's still shining"—running a horse plenty when he was in top form. Cannonade had won the Derby just seven days after winning the Stepping Stone Purse, a prep that had fallen into disfavor as other trainers decided a two- or three-week gap was preferable before the big race.

Woody had a low opinion of the horses that had made it to the 1982 Triple Crown and a high opinion of his own colt. Speed and quality would trump concerns about the five-day turnaround and the stretch-out from eight to 12 furlongs.

"A really good horse who can get a mile can get a mile and a half," he said matter-of-factly.

He couldn't wait for the Belmont and expected to win. The bettors still wanted to give Linkage another chance and made him the favorite, with Conquistador Cielo the second choice over Gato Del Sol and Aloma's Ruler. Heavy rain had turned the track sloppy, a final confusing factor.

At the time, bettors had few tools to refine their selections on wet tracks. The *Form's* only help was the somewhat haphazard awarding of "mud marks," large asterisks forever appended to the names of some horses who had won on "off" tracks. There were no career records for wet-track performances or published pedigree analyses suggesting which horses might be genetically inclined to run well in the rain.

Conquistador Cielo loved it. He cruised to the front, repelled a longshot's challenge, and opened the lead from a head after a mile to four lengths after 1¼ miles, winning by an astonishing 14 lengths as Gato Del Sol clunked up for second. Woody was cackling and crowing in the winner's circle.

The whole thing seemed bizarre to me and I didn't know what to make of it. Was Conquistador Cielo really 14 lengths better than the Kentucky Derby winner? Was this a truly great performance, or a case of one horse relishing a wet track and everyone else hating it? There was no question that Conquistador had one of the most amazing weeks in American racing history, setting the track record for a mile beating older horses on Monday and then winning the Belmont by 14 on Saturday. Still, I didn't know where this put him in the pantheon of racing's great ones.

Breeders had no such uncertainty, and for them the Belmont had an added dimension that made its winner seem like the conclusion of a long quest. Conquistador Cielo's sire, Mr. Prospector, had been a brilliant sprinter and already was considered a superior stallion who was always a good bet to pass on his quickness to his offspring. Breeders had been trying for years to blend that precocity with sturdiness and stamina, without much success, but here was a Mr. Prospector colt that had not only run the fastest mile in the history of Belmont Park but also had won the marathon among Triple Crown races.

That summer, as the yearling sales in Kentucky produced another round of soaring prices fueled by foreign investment, Conquistador Cielo was syndicated for a record $36.4 million—40 people paying nearly $1 million apiece for the right to breed a mare to him every year for as long as he lived. At season's end he would be retired to Claiborne Farm, the Hancock family's blue-chip Kentucky nursery where the stallions in residence included Secretariat and Mr. Prospector. Some breeders grumbled about the price tag but were afraid to pass up a chance at a potential sire for the ages. The shares sold quickly.

Conquistador Cielo kept running and making hay. He won the Dwyer Stakes by four lengths, and a month after that he tuned up for the Travers in the Jim Dandy, the traditional prep over the Saratoga track. He won by a diminishing length over the undistinguished Lejoli, but Woody insisted that his $36 million colt had been asked for only enough to win the race and get a feel for the track.

The Travers shaped up as something special because Gato Del Sol and Aloma's Ruler were running as well. It was the first time that separate winners of the Derby, Preakness, and Belmont had reunited for a sort of playoff in the Travers. Only two others joined them: Lejoli and the Canadian longshot Runaway Groom, seemingly in the race only because his owner had grown up near Saratoga.

Conquistador Cielo was a huge favorite at 2-5, but he never looked like a winner. He tussled with Aloma's Ruler for more than a mile but could never pull clear and the two of them turned for home exhausted. It seemed like a perfect set-up for Gato Del Sol, but he was trailing the field without advancing at all. Instead, it was the Canadian colt, Runaway Groom, who lumbered through a painfully slow final quarter-mile of 26 seconds to win by a half-length, with Aloma's Ruler holding second and Conquistador Cielo third.

The next morning, Conquistador was retired, officially due to an ankle injury he had suffered during the race. There were no protestations from Woody about how an unfortunate colt had been denied further greatness.

"We had a heck of a run with him," Woody said. "What am I supposed to do, go home and kill myself? I got a barn full of good 2-year-olds and we'll just try to find the next one."

The 1982 season was effectively over after a few whirlwind months. No one did anything noteworthy enough to dislodge Conquistador Cielo's performances as the year's best, and he was named both champion 3-year-old colt and Horse of the Year.

IT HAD BEEN an extraordinary first full season on the job, filled with several years' worth of drama and news, and I had no doubt that chronicling each season of racing was what I wanted to do for a long time. Yet I also had the growing feeling that I needed a more precise compass to get my bearings in this fascinating world.

My primitive work with breaking down fractional times in charts had given me a glimpse of objective certainty in a game that seemed ruled by opinions I could no longer trust. Perhaps the stories of the great horses of the past I had read and accepted as gospel were no more informed than the accounts of the contemporary sportswriters who described races with colorful clichés that flew in the face of the facts.

Conquistador Cielo had not accelerated and sprinted away from the field in the Belmont; he had run the first half of the race in 1:12 and the second half in 1:16⅘. Runaway Groom had not roared to a spectacular victory over a trio of brilliant classic winners in the Travers; he had outstaggered two exhausted pacesetters who were looking for a place to lie down.

I knew that fractions told another story, but they were only a small window affording an occasional insight, and they could be misleading too. It was obvious that a quarter-mile of 24 seconds might not mean the same thing at two different tracks, or even on the same track on different days of the week.

The *Form* had tried to address these issues with a "speed rating" and a "track variant," two small numbers in the past performances that, added together, were supposed to provide a universal guide to the quality of each race. Plenty of horseplayers seemed to swear by these numbers, but to me they were absurd. Conquistador Cielo had received a speed rating of 79 and a variant of 17 for a total of 96 in his Belmont triumph, and a rating of 86 and variant of 14 in his dreadful Travers for a higher total of 100. This was clearly ridiculous.

The methodology was so flawed as to be useless. The speed rating was based on how close each horse had come to the track record for that distance—equaling the track record earned a rating of 100, missing by one-fifth of a second was worth a 99, and so on. This at first sounds reasonable because it would appear to account for the fact that some surfaces are inherently faster than others.

The problem is that track records are usually set under freakishly fast temporary conditions and reflect one-time oddities of track maintenance rather than great performances by Hall of Famers. Many of the track records in existence were set by unremarkable horses rather than the finest performers in track history.

Also, tracks card races at a variety of distances, some of them rarely used, or never used for stakes races involving the best horses. So the same horse might earn a speed rating of 80 for running four full seconds slower than the track record at a commonly used distance and a 95 for running just one second slower at an odd distance. He had probably run about the same race, but the *Form* said one was 15 lengths better than the other.

The "variant," which was supposed to account for day-to-day differences in the quickness of any given track, could be just as misleading. It was an average of by how much all a day's races had missed the track record. The same track-record problems were part of this methodology, with the added complication that the variant often reflected only the caliber of horses running on any given card. On weekdays, when the cheapest races were held, the variant might be huge because the slowest horses on the grounds were running and missing the track record by a wide mark. On Saturday, when better races were run, including a stakes or two, the horses might be missing track records by a much slimmer margin—not because the surface was any faster, but because the quality of races that day was higher.

Without some way to account for all these factors, and to come up with a better method of measuring performance, I saw little potential growth for myself as either a horseplayer or as the person commemorating the deeds of America's best racehorses for the archives of *The New York Times*. I had gotten to the point as a player where I felt I could just about break even on a regular basis, but most races looked like crapshoots to me, and I felt no closer to solving them than I had been a year earlier.

Just as disturbing to me was the lack of any standard or system to measure horses in an absolute sense against history as well as in a relative sense against one another. How good had Conquistador Cielo really been? Was his Metropolitan truly the greatest mile ever run at Belmont Park?

In all the books I had read, only one person had tried to address these issues, and I had skipped over most of the specifics to enjoy his writing and tales of parimutuel derring-do. I now knew it was time to reread Andrew Beyer's *Picking Winners* and to see if speed figures were indeed, as he claimed, "the way, the truth, and the light."

One of the nice things about being a *Times* sportswriter was that you tended to work six- and seven-day weeks while your beat was in season, accumulating massive chunks of overtime that you were strongly encouraged to take as time off rather than extra pay. The previous year I had opted for the money, which meant having to work during the off-season. I had a brief and unhappy run covering hockey and college-football bowl games that erased any thoughts of becoming a general sports columnist.

So I took the time-off option for the winter of 1983 and spent most of it with an old copy of *Picking Winners* and a new IBM personal computer, a massive contraption that cost the entire $4,000 I had inherited from my great-aunt Mollie. I had spent virtually every Friday night of my childhood attending her mandatory weekly family dinners, where the herring and roast chicken were followed by two hours of cut-throat penny-ante poker. The game was the highlight of her week, so I decided that she would have appreciated my spending her bequest on gambling research.

I was determined not simply to learn and adopt Beyer's system, but to re-create and test all its assumptions and methods.

Beyer had popularized speed figures after figuring them out on his own, but had not invented them. Other handicappers of a previous generation—including Dave Wilson of the *Miami News*, Len Ragozin of "The Sheets" in New York, Pat Lynch of the old *World-Telegram*, and Russ Harris of the *Daily News*—had all formulated time-based systems for their personal use, but had never published them.

They, and probably some others who quietly did similar work, had independently come up with the same idea for stripping away track-to-track and day-to-day variations in order to recast final time in a form that allowed meaningful comparisons. The first step was to create a common language between distances, something known as a parallel time chart, so that instead of trying to compare raw times such as 1:12 for six furlongs and 1:25 for seven furlongs, you could say that those efforts were of equal quality and assign both performances a raw number of, say, 80.

The second step was to find the correct benchmark to compare against that effort—an expected or "par" time for that type of race to see if the track had been fast or dull that day. Beyer had provided a basic set of these crucial "par times," but I wanted both to verify them and to make them specific for New York racing nearly a decade later. The only way to do this was to build my own database, so I spent January doing nothing but typing three years of race results into the primitive version of a spreadsheet program called VisiCalc, entering the date, class, and final time of each of the 8,000 or so races that had been run in New York since January 1, 1980. Once I had entered all this data, I could then sort the races by class and distance, and use the result to create my own parallel time chart and pars.

I was the Strat-O-Matic scorekeeper again. When I was

finished, I not only had what I needed to start making my own speed figures, but also a new understanding of the fascinating hierarchy of Thoroughbred racing.

I had thought there were only four basic types of races: stakes events for the very best horses, allowance races for the next level, maiden races for newcomers in search of their first victory, and claiming races for runners past their prime. Now, though, I saw it didn't really work that way. There were dozens of gradations among these broad categories and far more overlap than I had assumed. Horses that appeared to be moving up or down in class might be doing the opposite. The *Form's* past performances were of little help because every allowance race was simply abbreviated to "Alw," with no reference to the dozen levels within the allowance ranks.

While the classes fell neatly into order over time, what was most startling was how often horses would run an unusually good race for that level and come back to win next time despite "moving up in class." Horseplayers routinely bet against such horses because they were "tackling tougher company." The horses didn't know the conditions of the races, though, and might well be meeting runners no faster than the ones they had just thrashed.

I began making my own daily speed figures and seeing races in an entirely new light. What had previously seemed like an inscrutable scramble now might look like an obvious case of one horse towering over the field. Heavy favorites might have no edge on my figures, and while such horses had once scared me, I now could take confident stands against them.

I was working in a vacuum, as no one published speed figures back then. I found a teacher and sounding board in Pat Lynch, who was retired from newspapers and a stint working at the New York tracks that had ended with a handshake agreement that he could have a seat in the press box for the rest of his life. When I returned to Aqueduct that spring after my winter of calculations, Lynch noticed that I was beginning my days the same way he did, going through the previous day's charts and scribbling a lot.

We began comparing figures, and I was relieved to find that ours were pretty close, not only because that meant there were probably no hideous flaws in my ciphering but also because I had come to admire Lynch's opinion. He would often knock the heavy favorite in a big race, saying the horse was no faster than anyone else, or opine that some forlorn-looking 15-1 shot was only a few inches slower than an opponent half his price. I had assumed Lynch had some goofy and flawed system that was leading him to these unorthodox pronouncements, but now I was coming to similar conclusions on my own.

It was like having a secret decoder ring to the *Form* while almost everyone else playing the game was staring at a foreign language and guessing at the words. Obviously there was more to handicapping than finding the fastest horse, but nothing was as basic and central to the entire proposition of racing.

The figures began to leap off the page at me when the 2-year-olds started racing that summer. Stakes and allowance races for 2-year-olds had always seemed particularly mysterious because every horse's past performances looked so similar, with practically every horse having won his debut. Bettors, and writers looking for the future stars of the class, tried to muddle through by comparing margins of victory and raw times or relying on visual impressions, but in many cases the speed figures showed there was one clearly superior horse.

That August, I missed the final Saturday of Saratoga in order to go cover Bates Motel, the country's top older horse, winning the Monmouth Handicap in New Jersey. I arrived back in Saratoga the next day and watched Capitol South win the Hopeful Stakes. A few people mentioned that Woody Stephens had won a maiden race the previous day with a good-looking first-time starter named Devil's Bag. When I did the weekend figures, I gave Capitol South a figure of 50 in the Hopeful and Devil's Bag a 51 in the maiden race he had won by 7½ lengths—nothing spectacular in and of itself, but still better than the year's first Grade 1 race for 2-year-olds.

(For those who wish to equate my speed figures with the current-day Beyers, my scale of numbers was three-fifths the size of his. My 40 equals a modern Beyer 67, a 50 is an 83, a 60 is a 100.)

Devil's Bag ran back eight days later, winning an allowance race in the slop and improving to a 54. Then a month later came the Cowdin Stakes at Belmont at seven furlongs. One of the other advantages to calculating my own figures was that I could make a preliminary variant for the day during the earlier races, so by the time the stakes was run at the end of the day, I could already project what the time of the race "should be" if the top-figure horse repeated his most recent number. The races leading up to the Cowdin were straightforward, and it looked as if Devil's Bag should cover the distance in around 1:22⅘ if he ran another 54.

He bolted to the lead as usual and won by three lengths, but what made my jaw drop was the final time: 1:21⅖. It was a stakes record and only one second off the track record, but, more amazing to me, it translated to an off-the-charts juvenile figure of 65, the equivalent of a modern Beyer of 109.

Was such a performance possible? I kept reviewing the day's times and variants and there was nothing to dispute it. Sometimes the track would speed up in the course of the day, necessitating a "split" variant, but this was a day when the races both before and after the Cowdin were solid and reliable.

Two weeks later in the Champagne, Devil's Bag won by six lengths stretching out to a mile and earned another 65. His time of 1:34⅕ was two to four seconds faster than older horses ran in other races on the card, and earned the same final figure as Slew o' Gold did winning the Jockey Club Gold Cup the same afternoon.

A couple of weeks later, I made one of my rare trips to the *Times*. One of the best parts of the job was that I spent all my time at the track and there was no reason to go to the office except for a twice-a-year lunch with my editors. We were supposed to be talking about my winter plans— hockey games or time off?—but all I could talk about was Devil's Bag. Sandy Padwe recalled that *Sports Illustrated* had once picked out a foal and followed him through the Kentucky Derby. What if I now did the same thing with Devil's Bag—followed him for the next six months, win or lose?

I needed all of five seconds to realize that this would require me to spend the entire winter in Florida and quickly accepted the assignment. On New Year's Day, I flew to Miami, grudgingly covered the Orange Bowl for the *Times,* then checked into a Holiday Inn for three months and began yet another educational odyssey. I had learned the game first through voracious reading and then from a winter of studying time and distance, and now would get an entirely different view by following a horse and his trainer around every day.

Devil's Bag was stabled at Hialeah Park, the most beautiful racetrack I had ever seen, a monument to tropical luxury with a Mediterranean-style clubhouse, endless marble stairways, a paddock area filled with statues and fountains, and a track infield inhabited by flamingos. The stable area was a serene

row of barns filled with New York's top horses on winter vacation, connected by soft dirt paths lined with towering pines.

Woody loved the idea of the *Times* series. He offered me
unlimited access to his employees and showed endless
patience with a city boy's awkwardness around a racing stable.
I showed up every morning to see Devil's Bag walk or gallop
and slowly learned how not to scare a horse or get stepped on
by one. Every two weeks I would file a long piece for the
Times that both chronicled Devil's Bag's progress and profiled
one of the people associated with him, learning the various
roles of an owner, breeder, trainer, jockey, exercise rider, hot-
walker, and groom.

Phil Gleaves, one of Woody's three assistants, became my
closest friend in the crew and he shared my awe of Devil's
Bag. An aspiring jockey in England before coming to America
in the hope of becoming a trainer, Gleaves had galloped the
colt since the day he had arrived in Woody's Belmont barn as
a 2-year-old and thought he was something truly extraordinary. In typical racetrack fashion, he had not revealed the
identity of the stable's hot 2-year-old to anyone until wising up
his closest friend the morning of the race.

"This is the day," Phil finally told him, "that the best horse
who has ever lived is going to run."

That same expectation surrounded Devil's Bag when he
made his 3-year-old debut in a seven-furlong tune-up for the
Flamingo, Hialeah's premier Derby prep. He had of course
been the 2-year-old champion and had fallen just short of
becoming the first 2-year-old since Secretariat to be named
the Horse of the Year as well. At season's end, he had been
weighted at 128 pounds on the Experimental Free Handicap,
a hypothetical year-end ranking of 2-year-olds, the highest
since Secretariat 11 years earlier. He also had been syndicat-

ed by Claiborne for $36 million, even though he had yet to race at 3.

Sent off at odds of 1-to-20 in a four-horse field, Devil's Bag romped to a seven-length victory in 1:21⅗ and earned a speed figure of 63. I was disappointed that he had run a smidge below his Cowdin and Champagne, but he had been off for almost four months and Woody had told me not to expect a peak performance the first time back. Not that there was anything wrong with a 63—and after all, it was still only February.

Eleven days later, the biggest crowd in Hialeah history turned out to see Devil's Bag in a high-quality Flamingo that also drew the other two fastest 3-year-olds in the East, Time for a Change and Dr. Carter. When the gates opened, Devil's Bag went to the lead along with Time for a Change and the two of them dueled through only moderate fractions over a very fast track. Devil's Bag put a nose in front turning for home and I waited for him to draw away. He didn't. Time for a Change pulled away from him and Devil's Bag couldn't keep up, surrendering second place to Dr. Carter in midstretch and even losing third to an undistinguished plodder named Rexson's Hope at the wire.

I was incredulous. After sending in a perfunctory paragraph on the result for the first edition, I hurried back to the barn, fully expecting to find that the colt had suffered an injury that would probably end his career. The good news was that there was nothing apparently wrong with him, but that was sort of bad news as well. No one could explain the performance.

Woody was disappointed but put the blame on himself for being overconfident and "babying" the colt. He was willing to throw out the race and start over. The next day, Phil Gleaves gave me the horseshoes Devil's Bag had worn in defeat, saying that someday they would make a historical curiosity because surely the Flamingo would turn out to be the only race he had ever lost.

Woody decided to take Devil's Bag to New York and run him in the Gotham Stakes and the Wood Memorial. Three weeks after the Flamingo debacle, Devil's Bag got on a cargo plane at Miami International Airport, accompanied by two grooms and a *New York Times* reporter.

Flying with the horse had seemed like a great idea for a story. I put my bags on the equipment van to New York and climbed into the horse van with Devil's Bag and three other horses who would share the flight, carrying only the big primitive portable computer the *Times* had begun issuing to reporters. On the way to the airport, a colt named Bihar took a healthy nip at my hand and banged open a swinging door with his nose. My computer went flying onto Okeechobee Road, never to recover.

Gleaves had told me to wear a jacket on the flight, which struck me as a curious dress code because I misinterpreted it to mean a blazer rather than a down-filled parka. So I spent the flight to New York freezing in the rear of a cargo plane, trying to write my story on the back of an envelope as my bitten hand swelled into an ugly red mess.

The next six weeks became a daily soap opera. Bad weather in New York forced the Gotham to be moved back a week. Woody broke three ribs in a household fall, then came down with pneumonia and was hospitalized. Claiborne brought in a former trainer named Mike Griffin, who was in charge of yearlings at the farm, to oversee the stable in Woody's absence.

Devil's Bag never ran in New York. Instead he went to Keeneland, where he raised hopes that the Flamingo had been a fluke with a 15-length victory in the Forerunner Purse that earned a sparkling 65. Woody still believed, and took a page from his playbook that he thought could make Devil's Bag a Derby winner: He would run him in the Derby Trial seven days before the main event, a strategy that had worked with Cannonade a decade earlier.

Two days before the Trial, Bill Nack from *Sports Illustrated* joined me for a 4:30 A.M. drive from Lexington to Louisville to see Devil's Bag's morning gallop. Nack had been Secretariat's similarly dedicated biographer, going so far as to sleep in the stable the night before the 1973 Belmont Stakes. As the twin spires of Churchill Downs came into view at dawn, it finally felt like there was going to be a Kentucky Derby with Devil's Bag in it after all.

Two days later, Devil's Bag won the Trial by 2¼ lengths and the world pronounced him the Derby favorite again, but now I knew that something was wrong. His figure fell off to a mediocre 58, seven points below what he had done at a mile six months earlier in the Champagne. Three days later, Claiborne's Seth Hancock visited Woody in the hospital and convinced him to skip the Derby. The official announcement was that the colt would now point for the Preakness, but Woody later told me the syndicate had decided to retire him even before a set of X-rays showed a tiny bone chip in one knee.

The Monday after the Derby, Devil's Bag was officially retired. Gleaves had been right: The Flamingo was the only race he had ever lost, though we had expected his subsequent victories to be more glorious than the Forerunner Purse and the Derby Trial.

The only thing stranger than watching the Derby that year without Devil's Bag in the gate was watching Woody win the race anyway. Swale, a Claiborne homebred whom Woody had always considered a likeably gritty colt but simply not in the same realm of talent as Devil's Bag, had quietly improved and matured that spring. He couldn't put two good races together, but he beat Dr. Carter by nearly a length to win the Florida Derby, earning a 60, and then caught a perfect set-up on Derby Day. Devil's Bag was out, Dr. Carter and Time for a Change both missed the race with viruses, and the favorite was a D. Wayne Lukas-trained filly named Althea who stopped badly after a mile. Swale admirably chugged along and won the Derby over a pair of longshots.

So I had spent months following the Derby-winning stable after all. I had just picked the wrong horse.

After throwing in a dreadful Preakness, Swale led all the way to give Woody his third straight Belmont, running a perfectly balanced race—his first six furlongs in 1:13⅗, the second six furlongs in the identical time for a final clocking of 2:27⅕ and a solid winning figure of 61. He lacked the brilliance of a Conquistador Cielo or Devil's Bag but could maintain a steady cruising speed.

A week after the Belmont, I arrived at the track to find that Swale had literally dropped dead that morning of heart failure, for no apparent reason. The stable crew snuck me into the autopsy that afternoon, and I dutifully reported the gruesome and ultimately fruitless procedure. It was the first column I wrote that the *Times* refused to print, on the grounds that it was "not appropriate breakfast-table reading." I was indignant at the time, but when I looked at it a few weeks later I couldn't blame them, since I couldn't read it myself without wincing.

Woody won the Belmont a fourth and then a fifth straight time over the next two years, the most astounding streak in racing history. Belmont built him a combination shrine and trophy case at the clubhouse entrance to the track, and in later years after Woody retired he would often linger there, regaling racegoers with his triumphs.

When I would see him and say hello, he would invariably introduce whoever was with him by saying that "Steve and I fought the battle of Devil's Bag." A few weeks before he died in 1998, Woody repeated his belief that Devil's Bag was the best 2-year-old anyone had ever trained and a better horse than any of his five Belmont winners. Twenty years later, no 2-year-old has put up two races as good as his Cowdin and Champagne, which today would earn Beyer figures in the 108-110 range.

I returned to Claiborne several times over the years to visit Swale's grave and look in on Devil's Bag and Conquistador Cielo. The two $36 million colts turned out to be decent but unspectacular sires, never replicating themselves but doing well enough that no one who paid around $1 million a share lost money. Not surprisingly, Conquistador Cielo's runners moved way up on sloppy tracks; his son Wagon Limit scored a massive upset in the mud in the Jockey Club Gold Cup. Devil's Bag's best offspring turned out not to be brilliant sprinters but solid middle-distance horses, such as Twilight Agenda and Devil His Due, and a number of grass horses with no early speed. Breeding is an inexact science.

So too, I had learned, were speed figures. They really were the way, the truth, and the light for measuring performance, separating contenders from pretenders, and uncovering horses who were much better or worse than they looked in the running lines. What they couldn't do was predict whether a horse would improve from 2 to 3 or stretch out from seven furlongs to a mile and an eighth and beyond.

The Devil's Bag series had opened my eyes to the fragility of horses and the behind-the-scenes dramas of racing. It also got me a raise and a well-meaning offer from my editors. It had been a long six months and maybe I needed a freshener—how would I like to go to the Olympics in Los Angeles for a month and write offbeat columns and feature stories? Wasn't it time for me to think about a sportswriting career beyond racing?

My response disappointed them: I had no interest in sports beyond racing, and if the Olympics conflicted with Saratoga, I couldn't possibly go. They looked at me as if I had two heads and we never discussed it again.

They were right about my being burned out, but I had never been happier. The Devil's Bag experience had drawn me deeply inside the game, and the figures had given me a magical tool to unlock many of its secrets. The fact that it did not reveal them all only deepened the attraction. Horse races were largely quantifiable, but there would always be more than enough mystery and ambiguity to demand imaginative thinking as well as mathematical analysis.

More important, I had fallen in love, and not just with the game.

For more than a year I had been freelancing a weekly roundup of New York racing for *The Thoroughbred Record,* a trade magazine based in Kentucky. As usual I wrote my pieces as close to deadline as possible, and the managing editor, Robin Foster, would call me twice every Tuesday, first demanding to know where my story was, and then later to point out errors and omissions in my copy. She was usually right about everything, except when it came to Devil's Bag and Swale. She had taken a shine to the latter as a 2-year-old and I spent the next six months patiently explaining to her that Swale wasn't fast enough to win the Kentucky Derby.

So I congratulated her the night of the Derby, and consoled her on our second date, the night of the Preakness. A few months later she moved to New York and we have been together ever since.

KING OF THE PICK SIX

I WAS SPOILED BY having spent an entire winter in Florida, and resolved to convince the *Times* that this should become a permanent arrangement. I argued that all the good horses from New York wintered there and I was more likely to find the Derby winner at Hialeah or Gulfstream than on the all-weather inner track at Aqueduct.

Andy Beyer, who long ago had sold his editors on a similar set-up, proved a useful example: If the editors of *The Washington Post* thought it was worthwhile for their racing writer to spend the high season in Florida, shouldn't *The New York Times* do the same? Surprisingly, the *Times* agreed.

Beyer and I had become friendly once I started making my

own figures. We could now discuss racing in the same language and commiserate about the frequent difficulties of calculating figures at Gulfstream, where mysterious forces seemed to make it especially hard to crunch running times into numbers. Some people theorized that the nearby ocean tides were to blame. For whatever reason, the quickness of the Gulfstream surface could change several times a day. There weren't many people around with whom one could discuss whether the variant should be switched from 8 to 15, and before the fourth as opposed to the fifth race.

There was a new bet that winter in Florida, imported from California. It was called the pick six, and required you to select the winners of six straight races in advance. Its unique feature was that this task frequently proved impossible for anyone. When that happened there would be a small "consolation" payout to those who had picked five of six winners, but 75 percent of the pool would "carry over" to the next day's racing. If the bet went unhit for two or more days, the carryover pool could climb toward $100,000.

Many small bettors regarded the pick six as the equivalent of playing the lottery and either ignored it or made a single $2 ticket, just in case today was the luckiest day of their lives. The way the bet really worked, for those with bigger bankrolls, was to use more than one horse per race and cover as many of the likeliest winners as you could afford.

It quickly got expensive. Using two horses per race cost $128 (2 x 2 x 2 x 2 x 2 x 2 = 64 x $2=$128), but three per race zoomed to $1,458, and four per race skyrocketed to $8,192. The trick seemed to be to select one or two races where you were willing to stand alone with one or maybe two horses, and spread out a bit more in the tougher events. A ticket that went

3 x 1 x 2 x 4 x 2 x 6, for example, would cost $576 and offer a decent chance of winning if you had picked the right horses in the races where you had narrowed things down.

I was finally winning more often than losing, thanks to my speed figures, but was grinding out only a modest profit rather than ever being in position to make a big score. When Beyer asked me to join a small group he had put together to share the cost of playing the pick six, I happily accepted. Beyer would bankroll about half the ticket, with smaller shares allotted to team members including Joe Cardello and Mark Hopkins, his figure-making partners, and Paul Cornman, a full time horseplayer with outstanding race-watching skills.

The four of them roomed together for the season and would share their opinions and negotiate a ticket at home, then Beyer and I would sit down at the track the next day after any scratches were announced and I would try to talk him into or out of any horses about which I had differing opinions. My primary value to the team seemed to be based less on anyone's high regard for my brilliant handicapping insights than on my knack for quickly calculating the cost of the tickets and suggesting strategies to include more horses.

The structure of the pick six had immediately clicked with my math skills and compulsive mental ordering of things. I instantly knew how much a ticket would cost by glancing at it. While multiplying six small numbers was no great challenge, figuring the cost and makeup of a ticket became a lot more complicated with the added twist of what Beyer termed "main" and "backup" tickets.

A basic pick-six ticket, such as the $576 play that went 3 x 1 x 2 x 4 x 2 x 6, might look something like this:

Race A:	1,3,5
Race B:	7
Race C:	2,4
Race D:	3, 6, 9, 12
Race E:	5,8
Race F:	4,6,7,8,9,11

The fact that our group could invest $576 gave us a huge edge against those trying to play by themselves for $128 or less by using only one or two horses per race. Beyer was willing to stand alone with those one or two horses in some spots, but other races were so contentious or inscrutable that he wanted to go even deeper. In the ticket above, he might want additional coverage with three more horses in Race D and four more in Race F, but simply adding those to the ticket would nearly triple its cost to $1,680.

This led to the idea of backup tickets. The strategy was to winnow those two tough races even further and classify a small number of the horses as mains and the rest as backups. Here's how it worked:

	Mains	Backups
Race A:	1,3,5	
Race B:	7	
Race C:	2,4	
Race D:	3, 6,	8,9,10,11,12
Race E:	5,8	
Race F:	4,6	1,2,3,5,7,8,9,11

Instead of putting in a single ticket, you would now put in three different tickets as follows:

	Ticket 1	Ticket 2	Ticket 3
Race A:	1,3,5	1,3,5	1,3,5
Race B:	7	7	7
Race C:	2,4	2,4	2,4
Race D:	3,6	8,9,10,11,12	3,6
Race E:	5,8	5,8	5,8
Race F:	4,6	4,6	1,2,3,5,7,8,9,11
Ticket cost:	$96	$240	$384

Ticket 1 was a skinnied-down version of the original $576 ticket and consisted of just the "main" horses. Ticket 2 was the "backup Race D" ticket, using five additional horses in that race. One of them was allowed to win, but then we would have only two horses in Race F. On Ticket 3, though, if one of the skinnied-down mains from Race D won, we would now have 10 horses going for us in the finale—the two mains on Ticket 1, and eight backups on Ticket 3. We had added a total of seven more horses to the play, but the cost had gone up only from $576 to $720 ($96 + $240 + $384).

What we were basically doing was creating a sort of old-time Chinese-restaurant menu and saying that we were allowed either six selections from Column A or five from Column A and one from Column B. You could only have one backup horse win, and if he did, "A's" had to win the other five races. There were countless ways to structure the tickets and as many scenarios for suffering heartbreaking losses. The last-minute designation of a horse as a B rather than an A could leave you with all the winners of a $100,000 pick six somewhere on your three tickets, but not all six on any one of them.

As the majority partner, Beyer made the final calls on the play, and the unwritten rule was that once the tickets had been bought, no whining or recriminations were permitted. I also learned that being part of the team meant being part of no other team.

One day I tried to talk Beyer into using Clock Tower, a longshot in a maiden race, but despite my recitation of his subtle virtues, Beyer would not include the horse. It was the day of a big carryover, and Steve Nagler, a friend of mine from California who was an aspiring racing-television producer, was visiting Gulfstream for the day. He suggested we put in a small ticket together and we quickly collaborated on a play prominently featuring Clock Tower.

We all got through the first three legs of the bet, two of which broke the best way and were won by long-priced horses. Then came the Clock Tower race, and he got up in the last jump to win at 18-1 over a decent-priced main from the Beyer team's ticket. Beyer graciously came over, deflated from the narrow miss on what was now shaping up as a huge payoff, and told me he wished he had allowed me to sway him.

"Well," I told him, "if you still have the heart to root for me and Nagler, we put in a little ticket of our own and we're alive."

Beyer asked me who we needed in the remaining two legs and walked off. We were knocked out in the next race, by a horse the team had used and Steve and I had not, and we both had the last winner. No one had the pick six, but the five-of-six consolations, which both groups had, made it a profitable afternoon.

Beyer usually held on to any consolation money for the next day's play, paying dividends only if we hit a big one. But now he walked over and handed me my share of that day's proceeds. He told me I had committed a "serious breach of gambling etiquette" by investing separately in the pick six after discussing the card with him and knowing the team's ticket. He said that he and the team had spent the last two races "rooting against you with every bone in our bodies."

It all blew over within a week and our partnership resumed for the winter, culminating with a $60,000 hit at Hialeah that March, 10 percent of which went to me. The blowup had been a good lesson in how things can change when gambling stakes reach a high level and also opened my eyes to a competitiveness in horseplaying that I intellectually knew existed but hadn't fully appreciated. Especially in the sort of private poker game of the pick six, this really was a contest among the customers, not a band of brothers playing against the house.

THE PICK SIX had completely captured my imagination on several different levels. One of the great things about the racetrack is that every day the game begins anew and with unlimited promise, the chance that this is the day all your opinions will be right. Every horseplayer, though, can find ways to squander such days, betting good opinions the wrong way, and going home with only a token profit or even a loss on a day when his pockets should be stuffed with cash. The pick six offered a single goal and challenge, a contest involving most of the afternoon's races.

For all the complexity of constructing a ticket, the bet actually simplified my day at the races. Instead of constantly checking the odds board and agonizing over which races to play and how to bet them, I could now just put in my pick-six tickets early in the day and then write or work relatively undistracted, taking a break each half hour to watch a race and root to stay alive.

Playing the pick six also meant handicapping in advance

more carefully than ever, since you couldn't skip a race in the sequence and you had to look at every horse closely and designate him as a main, a backup, or a throw-out. The bet forced me to examine each race and horse and hone my speed figures even more sharply.

I was wedding myself to a full set of daily record-keeping tasks. You couldn't skip analyzing and recording a single day's results because each card of racing produced figures for 80 or 90 individual horses that would run back in the weeks ahead. It was a level of detail an outsider might consider obsessive, if not pathologically insane, but I truly enjoyed it. Stationery supplies became a minor fetish as I sought out the smallest and sharpest felt-tipped pens to inscribe my records into the tiny grids in my graph-paper notebooks.

The pick six came to New York that summer and I was ready to attack it seriously on my own. I was willing to take on partners but was determined to keep the group small and to be the ultimate decision-maker. I recruited two friends as 20 percent partners each—Nagler and Rich Rosenbush, a *Times* copy editor who usually handled my stories because he was one of the few sports-department employees who knew and liked racing. We decided we needed a total stake of $10,000, so Steve and Rich each put up $2,000. To prevent any misunderstandings, we even executed a written agreement covering payouts and exclusivity and stipulating that the decisions of The Syndicate Manager would be final.

While playing with the Beyer team that winter, I had realized that there was even greater potential in the main/backup system than the simple version we had used. Rather than buying backup tickets in two races a day, what if you had backups and contingencies in virtually every race? Instead of demanding that your Chinese menu consist of six A's or five A's and one B, what if you could construct a more elaborate dinner in which you could get four items from Column A and up to two from Column B? Might there even be a Column C, exotic side horses you could add to the menu if everything else worked out perfectly?

The nuisance factor in this approach was making out so many tickets—usually at least 10 and as many as 30 with a particularly complicated play. You had to bet the pick six by filling out special cards, inking in the numbers of the horses in each leg as if you were marking the answer sheet on a standardized test. What made all the paperwork tolerable was knowing that no one else was approaching the bet this way and that all the permutations had to give us an edge.

I would handicap the card in great detail each night and then consult with my partners the following morning. Rich was a skeptic and contrarian thinker who would force me to justify my selections, and he would occasionally come up with an interesting horse I had overlooked. Nagler's opinions were more difficult to assimilate because he had fallen under the influence of The Sheets, Len Ragozin's $25-a-day speed figures, which had a small but cultlike following. In an era when they were the only alternative to making your own, they were better than no speed figures at all, but The Sheets modified their figures in ways I didn't trust.

First, they were raised or lowered depending on how much weight a horse had carried, then adjusted again to reflect whether the horse had raced on the inside or the outside of the track. Finally, they were arrayed in vertical columns on a sheet of graph paper, and the patterns they formed were supposed to suggest predictable improvements or regressions in the horse's form.

So Nagler would want to use horses that The Sheets said

were just as fast as my pure top-figure horses because they had carried more weight or raced wide or because their figures on the graph were pointing in a favorable direction. Each day became a protracted negotiation, and when we failed to hit anything while running through half of our $10,000, he bowed out. A week later, Rich and I hit for $27,000. Steve never complained and we have remained close friends, arguing to this day about the validity of Sheets methodology.

Even having just one partner was not without its frustrations. What do you do when a 20 percent shareholder has just one passionate opinion on a card and you couldn't disagree with it more? In the 1985 Breeders' Cup at Aqueduct, Rich's horse of the day was Track Barron in the Classic, and I didn't think the colt could get a mile and a quarter without assistance from a tow truck. I bowed to his fervor, demoted the ultimately victorious Proud Truth to a backup, and we missed a score. The following summer I rejected his insistence that the front-running Groovy could hold off Turkoman in the Forego Handicap at Saratoga, singled Turkoman, and am reminded by him at least annually of Groovy's desperate victory.

I was doing my betting and cashing in the press box, and soon almost all of my colleagues wanted to play along and take a piece of my action. It seemed like a good idea at the time, if only for some camaraderie with the people in whose company I was spending eight hours a day, six times a week. Unlike the generalists and columnists who showed up for the big races, the New York press-box crew in those days was a genial group of eccentrics who thoroughly enjoyed the game and the beat. Most of them were enthusiastic but small-scale bettors who couldn't afford to play the pick six on their own, but for $5 or $10 they could buy 1 percent of my usual $500 to $1,000 daily ticket.

These arrangements quickly grew out of control. It was fine when half a dozen colleagues were taking a point or two each, but soon the elevator operator and the griddle cook and the summer intern running the mimeograph machine all wanted to play along too. People didn't understand that it wasn't fair to ask for a piece only when there was a big carryover, since they hadn't been part of my losing tickets the previous two or three days. The bookkeeping alone became practically a full-time job, requests for credit were commonplace, and worst of all, I had to listen to 12 people's opinions every day.

I finally instituted a rule that those who wanted a piece had to take the same percentage every day, give me the money in advance and, most important, were not allowed to discuss the races with me. They could come over and copy down the tickets before the first leg of the pick six, but risked permanent expulsion by commenting on my selections or strategy.

That did not preclude second-guessing after the results were in, which could be brutal. One especially excruciating beat involved a day when I was in position to take an entire $342,000 carryover pool after my intricate array of tickets had weaved its way through several longshots, leaving me with only the favorite in the final leg. He was narrowly beaten by a perfectly logical 3-1 shot who was the second choice in the race, a horse I would have had as well had things broken just slightly differently.

Russ Harris, the handicapper for the *Daily News,* proudly came over to me after the race and pointed out that he had picked that winner in the paper. "We really should have talked!" he said cheerfully.

No jury of horseplayers would have convicted me had I strangled him on the spot, but somehow I restrained myself.

Missing $342,000 pick sixes perhaps should have been

more traumatic for someone making $42,000 a year, but strange as it may sound, playing the pick six never seemed primarily about the money. It was about doing all the intricate work in advance and the fun and challenge of playing in a tournament every day. The money was off to the side, a bankroll entirely separate from a paycheck and living expenses. If I held a lone winning ticket worth $40,000 on a non-carryover day, it was just as exciting to know that I was the only person at the track who had come up with the correct sequence as it was to collect the payoff.

There was always less cash to show for a winning season than there should have been, thanks to an absurd and unjust Internal Revenue Service policy about gambling proceeds that persists to this day. Most civilized countries don't tax gambling winnings at all, but even an American horseplayer perfectly willing to be an honest citizen and pay an income tax on his actual profit for the year faces an intermediate hurdle that can break him. The IRS requires that 20 percent of gross proceeds be withheld from any payoff of more than 300-1, and at the time, New York State took another 8 percent on top of that.

So if I hit a $10,000 pick six, $2,000 would come off the top for the Feds and another $800 went to the state, leaving me with $7,200. It didn't matter if I had lost $10,000 over the previous month, or even that I might have invested $1,000 that day and thus had only received a return of 9-1, much less than the 300-1 threshold. The IRS pretended that I had made a single winning $2 bet, was $9,998 ahead for the year, and that it and the state were now entitled to withhold 28 percent of my gross return.

No other business enterprise or form of income in the world is treated this way. Imagine if your local grocer had to turn over 28 cents to the government from each $1 sale, right on the spot. His store would be shuttered in a month.

You could claim losses against winnings when you did your taxes at the end of the year, as long as you kept careful records and were prepared for an audit (I've survived two), but by then you might be a broke winner. Suppose that in 1986, I bet $200,000 and hit $230,000 worth of pick sixes. I was grudgingly willing to say that the government deserved a piece of my $30,000 profit, but it had already confiscated $64,400 from my winnings, leaving me $34,400 out of pocket, nearly my gross annual income.

I repeatedly tried to interest my former colleagues on the *Times* editorial page in the issue, without success. Neither they nor track officials, some of them people with strong political connections, considered it a cause worth taking up. They would chuckle and respond that the cash-flow problems of gamblers were hardly a legitimate public-policy concern (as opposed to, say, capital-gains tax breaks for wealthy financiers). It was another reminder of society's low esteem for people who wager, and an eye-opener to me about how far removed the people running the sport were from their best customers.

While my entrée to racing had been as a grandstand bettor, it somehow hadn't occurred to me during my first few years on the beat that the customers were as much a part of the game as the participants I regularly sought out in the stable area and quoted in the *Times*. It was such a captivating world that I felt lucky to have found it and become a part of it, but more and more I was beginning to think that the regular bettors were generally getting a raw deal, and not just when it came to tax-withholding policy.

Writing for the *Times* didn't give me much of a dialogue with the daily customers. A few of them might have had the paper delivered at home, and the Wall Street contingent who gambled on horses as well as the market read me regularly, but the *Times* wasn't even sold at the track. Most of my readers were weekend enthusiasts rather than regular players, or participants at the highest level of the sport—owners, breeders, and officials.

Then Harvey Pack, who hosted New York's nightly race-replay show, *Thoroughbred Action,* on SportsChannel, began to expose me to a new and different audience from my *Times* readers by making me a regular guest on the show. Most of his guests would belabor the obvious as they talked over the stretch runs of the replays, saying it had been an exciting race or that the winner might be a good horse because he had won by many lengths. Making my own figures in the midst of each card turned out to be a boon, because I could say on the same day the races had been run whether a race had been fast or slow for this grade of horse and could calibrate whether that easy winner had in fact run a stakes-class number or was merely an ordinary horse beating up on a bad field.

On days that I was Harvey's guest, he would take a point or two of my pick-six action and narrate the card with constant references to my ticket—"Crist got his single home in here," or "The gentleman from the *Times* went five deep in this race and still managed to miss the winner!" The audience enjoyed the vicarious action, especially when I suffered a wrenching beat with which they could identify. After a run at Saratoga in 1987 during which I hit the bet six times in eight days, Harvey christened me the King of the Pick Six, and the moniker stuck.

Harvey also hosted an open-air handicapping seminar each day at Saratoga, where his guest would deliver a 20-minute monologue going through all the day's races. One day when there was a carryover, I breezed through the card as usual and then recapped it by outlining how I would play the pick six if

I were making out just a single ticket and spending only $96. The theoretical play hit for over $13,000, and about three times as many people as the number of announced winners subsequently thanked me for the score.

The very minor celebrity of appearing on a local replay show reached its most unexpected point when Robin and I were married in June of 1987 and honeymooned in England and Scotland. Among the highlights of the trip (besides betting on greyhounds jumping over little fences at Powderhall, the dog track in Edinburgh) was the afternoon we were visiting the Tower of London and another tourist shouted out from across a cobbled courtyard, "Hey Steve Crist! I watch you on the Harvey Pack show!"

My appearances with Harvey had given me recognition well beyond the scope of the *Times*, and I found more and more customers approaching me around the track to discuss betting and to share their gripes and grievances about the game. I started soliciting such encounters by making a lazy walk though the track part of my daily routine, and I began to see that racing was falling farther and farther behind customer-service expectations that had been raised by the quiet growth of alternative forms of gambling over the past decade.

Track attendance was declining steadily while the Atlantic City casinos were booming. For those who just wanted gambling action, the casinos were an easy choice—less work, bigger jackpots to chase, glitzier surroundings. Even the bettors who had remained loyal to racing because of the mental challenge of handicapping and the prospect of victory through skill now expected better treatment, or at least some recognition that they were valued customers whose patronage was appreciated. At the casinos, players were rewarded with free food and drinks and, if they bet enough, floor-show tickets and hotel suites as well. A horseplayer got nothing, not even an occasional sandwich or a thank-you.

They also got a view of racing from the *Form* that I would increasingly come to believe was irrelevant at best and deceptive at worst. Betting was rarely even mentioned and there were never any articles about handicapping or speed figures or customer service. Other than Joe Hirsch's encyclopedic legwork, what passed for news was little more than rewritten press releases from the tracks, even as the sport was rocked by change in the second half of the 1980's.

MY FIRST FEW years on the racing beat had been all about the horses and the racing, or at least that's how I had chosen to see and cover it. There was a comforting sameness to the racing calendar and to my itinerary: the 3-year-olds would sort themselves out in Florida over the winter, then everyone would move on to Kentucky, Baltimore, and New York for the five-week pressure cooker of the Triple Crown. Saratoga followed soon thereafter, and then came the Belmont fall meeting, where big races every weekend would crown the divisional champions and the Horse of the Year.

The game had undergone little true progress in a generation, but in the mid-80's suddenly that all began to change. It was a great time to be a reporter, especially for a New York paper, because New York's long-standing dominance of American racing was in the crosshairs of transition.

The Breeders' Cup, first run in 1984, had instantly transformed the championship structure of the game. It was a brilliant idea, though few believed in it when it was first announced that a prominent Kentucky breeder, John Gaines, had proposed a series of seven year-end races worth a total of

$10 million. Instead of relying on the ancient races of the "Fall Championship Meeting" at Belmont to settle titles on a succession of lazy autumn afternoons, the Breeders' Cup would compress everything into a four-hour Thoroughbred Olympics held at a different venue each year.

Gaines got the owners and breeders, flush from the bloodstock boom, to agree to help fund the races and convinced NBC to televise a racing broadcast that was three times as long as had ever been aired. He also was insistent that the inaugural Cup be held in California, to lend some Hollywood sparkle to the event and win the loyalty of the California racing community, which often felt isolated from the sport's New York-Kentucky axis of power.

The inaugural Cup at Hollywood Park in 1984 went by in a giddy blur. Never before had so many top horses been assembled at a single site to run on the same afternoon, and by day's end, the only question was why no one had thought of it sooner.

The following spring the sport's other great event, the Triple Crown, came under fire from an unlikely source. Robert Brennan, a slick-talking securities salesman with a passion for horses and high-stakes gambling, had purchased Garden State Park, a faltering old track in central New Jersey, and remade it in the image of the glittering new casinos an hour away in Atlantic City. To draw attention to the new plant, Brennan enriched the purses for two minor Derby preps and offered a series of outlandish bonuses for winning various combinations of those two races, the Kentucky Derby, and the track's traditional Memorial Day race, the Jersey Derby.

Few serious Kentucky Derby candidates had emerged from Garden State in decades, and the Jersey Derby had become a forgotten race for 3-year-olds a cut below Triple Crown quality. That spring, however, a freakishly fast front-runner named

Spend a Buck rocketed to victories in the two preps and then led every step of the way to win the Derby.

The colt's connections now had to choose between trying for the Triple Crown and shooting for a $2 million bonus in the Jersey Derby, and they chose the latter. He won the race and the bonus by a neck and was retired after one more victory. By the end of an otherwise lackluster racing reason, Spend a Buck had done enough to be the Horse of the Year.

For the second time in four seasons, the Derby winner had skipped the Preakness, and the shaky future of the Triple Crown forced its host tracks to join the world of progressive sports promotion. Purses for the races were hiked, bonuses were instituted for participating in all three events, and Churchill, Pimlico, and Belmont formed Triple Crown Productions to market and publicize the series.

Another agent of change was D. Wayne Lukas. He was just emerging on the national scene when he won the 1980 Santa Anita Derby with Codex, but by decade's end he had personally revolutionized the training game.

Lukas came from the world of Quarter Horse racing, where he had rewritten that sport's record books through strength in numbers, cornering the market on top prospects. No one had tried to do the same at the top level of Thoroughbred racing, but Lukas thought the sport was ripe for picking. American racing offered rich stakes races at tracks all over the country every weekend, and outside of the very biggest events, these races were won by the best of the local horses at each track. Lukas saw an opportunity not only to have a division of horses at every major venue in the country, but also to exploit increasingly available and affordable air travel to execute raids on a national scale.

Backed by deep-pocketed owners including Texas oilmen and Eugene Klein, the owner of the San Diego Chargers, Lukas began sending precocious 2-year-olds all over the country for the prime local events. In the past, a California or New York trainer would run an impressive maiden winner back in an allowance race or two before trying a stakes race. Lukas would forgo the $30,000 allowance race to put a horse on a plane to Nebraska or Illinois for a $75,000 stakes race. "D. Wayne off the plane" became a handicapping byword and angle.

Other trainers, especially the old-timers, raged that Lukas was more of a manager than a true horseman, and he always had a rocky relationship with most of the racing press, which found his methods and manner abrasive. I had hit it off well with him from the start, writing a long piece for the *Times* about Landaluce, a spectacular 2-year-old filly he trained in 1982. When she died from an infection two months later, the *Times* had put my obituary of her on the front page of the paper on a slow news day.

As Lukas set new records for earnings and stakes victories nearly every season, he continued to be challenged about the remaining gaps on his resume. He ran horses in the Derby every year, and his failure to win the race with his first 12 starters was cited as proof that he couldn't succeed on the game's biggest stage. He finally broke through with a vengeance when he sent out the filly Winning Colors to win the race in 1988. The beef then turned to his supposed inability to train older horses and grass runners, but he made champions of Criminal Type and Steinlen.

Lukas's operation was national but his home base was California, which was growing ever more influential in other ways. Having three of the first four Breeders' Cups there had lent a previously absent championship quality to its fall racing, and in the second half of the 1980's it became the launching pad for Kentucky Derby winners: Ferdinand in 1986, Alysheba in 1987, Winning Colors in 1988, and Sunday Silence in 1989 all came out of California.

New York's primacy had been toppled and it was turning into a minority in another key aspect of the game: medication. As year-round racing had become commonplace in revenue-hungry jurisdictions in the late 1970's and the 1980's, horsemen had successfully lobbied for the legalization of two race-day medications they claimed were necessary to keep horses in training: the anti-inflammatory phenylbutazone, known as Bute, and the diuretic furosemide, better known under the trade name Lasix, used to treat horses who would get blood in their windpipes from the strain of racing.

Lasix became a volatile issue in the sport, further polarizing New York from the rest of the country. Supporters claimed it was purely a humane treatment, while opponents said it was unnecessary for most horses and was being used to flush illegal substances out of their systems. Studies of large samples of horses showed that their performance usually improved when treated with Lasix for the first time—but did that mean it was a performance-enhancer, a mask for other "hops," or simply an effective way to get horses to run to their full ability?

The Lasix issue dominated the career of Alysheba, who won the 1987 Derby and Preakness, becoming the first horse since Pleasant Colony in 1981 to be one race away from winning the Triple Crown. The son of Alydar had raced in Kentucky and Maryland with Lasix but was not permitted to use it in New York, and when he was trounced by nearly 15 lengths in the Belmont, the Lasix critics grew only more convinced that New York was the game's last bastion of purity.

I was relieved when Alysheba lost the Triple Crown, simply because at the time he didn't seem brilliant or accomplished enough to join the immortals. He had brought a record of just

1 for 10 into the Derby and had never run a particularly fast race. His apparent inability to win without Lasix seemed like a third strike. The following year as a 4-year-old, though, Alysheba turned into a faster and more consistent horse, and to me, the crowning moment of his career was when he returned to New York and ran without Lasix while winning an excellent Woodward Stakes.

I had pressed the issue throughout the colt's career, practically unable to write a story about Alysheba without discussing his use of Lasix. When I saw his owner, Clarence Scharbauer, approaching me a couple of weeks after the Woodward, I prepared to congratulate him and braced myself for a scolding, but he spoke first and was more gracious than I could have imagined.

"I want to thank you for writing about Lasix," he said, "because it made us want to prove he could win without it."

Alysheba closed out his career in the Breeders' Cup Classic at Churchill Downs on an afternoon that many fans still believe was the best day of racing they have ever seen. Alysheba capped it by emerging from virtual darkness in cold, drizzly conditions to win the Classic by a half-length. Earlier in the day, an even more dramatic career had come to a close when Personal Ensign became the first major champion in 80 years to complete a literally perfect career. She had won all 12 of her previous starts but looked hopelessly beaten turning for home in the Breeders' Cup Distaff before launching an impossible late run that carried her to a narrow victory over Lukas's Derby winner, Winning Colors.

That Breeders' Cup card also included the defeat of a colt I had fallen for completely, the fastest 2-year-old since Devil's Bag. Easy Goer, another son of Alydar, was a bit shy of the Devil's figures, but this was a colt I knew would only get better as the distances got longer. A big horse with a long stride, he rallied from off the pace and finished with a flourish. As I watched him win the Cowdin and the Champagne by widening margins I could already picture him completing the Triple Crown over the same Belmont track eight months later.

Easy Goer was the quintessential New York horse, bred and owned by the Phipps family, which had long been a ruling force in the operation of New York's tracks and The Jockey Club, the registry of the breed and standard-bearer for tradition in the sport. Ogden Phipps, the patriarch of the clan, was nearly 80 but still was regularly driven to the stables to inspect his horses and rarely missed a big day at the track. His son, Ogden Mills "Dinny" Phipps, had been chairman of the New York tracks and The Jockey Club and a prime mover in funding equine research.

Outside New York, the Phippses were viewed warily at best, and were seen as symbols of the Eastern power and privilege that had once ruled the game with a heavy hand. Perhaps I overlooked all that, being a defender of most things New Yorkish, but I also liked both of them. One of my favorite afternoons as a reporter was spent with Ogden Phipps at his Long Island estate, looking through the scrapbooks he could no longer read and listening to his stories about the great Thoroughbreds his family had bred and raced, such as Bold Ruler and Buckpasser. He cited from memory things I had written about his horses. I wondered how he had seen them, and Dinny later told me he would read my columns to his father at the breakfast table.

Easy Goer was trained by Shug McGaughey, who had managed Personal Ensign's career so perfectly and was emerging as the logical successor to Woody Stephens as New York's premier trainer. With clients such as the Phippses and Claiborne Farm, Shug figured to have a long career training good horses, but he already suspected that Easy Goer might be a once-in-a-lifetime colt.

Easy Goer returned even bigger and stronger in the spring of 1989, winning his three Derby preps with commanding ease, and headed to Churchill Downs the heaviest Derby favorite in a decade. Only one horse appeared to stand in his way: Sunday Silence, a racy, nearly black colt trained by Charlie Whittingham, California's version of Woody in longevity and success. Whittingham was perfectly happy doing almost all of his racing in California and regularly passed up the Triple Crown, preferring to allow his horses to mature slowly. That he was at Churchill Downs at all for only the third time since 1960 said a lot about what he thought of his colt's chances.

I refused to allow the possibility that two colts as good as Easy Goer could have come from the same foal crop. Could racing really have another Affirmed and Alydar? The similarities were striking. Sunday Silence, like Affirmed, was a California-based front-runner of moderate breeding and nimble athleticism. Easy Goer, like his sire, was a blue-blooded stretch-runner with a legitimately strong finishing kick.

They played their roles to depressing perfection in the Derby and Preakness. In Kentucky, Sunday Silence seized the lead turning for home and Easy Goer came running with too little too late. Still, Easy Goer was the heavy Preakness favorite, but was simply outdueled to the wire in a long drive. That bitter defeat turned much of the public and press against a colt who only a month earlier they had thought might be the next Secretariat.

In a *USA Today* poll of racing writers on the eve of the Belmont, almost everyone went for Sunday Silence; Beyer, once as great a fan of Easy Goer as I still was, felt so betrayed that he picked Sunday Silence to win by 12 lengths. A *Times* sports columnist referred to Easy Goer as "a creation of the New York media," a rare dig at a colleague. Sunday Silence was the odds-on choice, Easy Goer 8-5 after going off as a heavy favorite in all 11 previous starts.

About the only press-box supporters Easy Goer still had were "the New York media," the handful of regular writers and handicappers for the New York papers who were now badly outnumbered by a national corps of general columnists expecting to see racing's next Triple Crown winner.

Belmont Day seemed to drag on forever, even though I got a few longshots home in the early legs of a pick six that would culminate in the Belmont Stakes. I kept trying to convince myself that we hadn't seen the real Easy Goer in Kentucky and Maryland, and that back on his home court, he could still be the colt I thought he had been and avenge his sire's heart-breaking loss 11 years earlier. If he didn't, if Sunday Silence edged him again, then at least Sunday Silence was more than worthy to become the 12th Triple Crown winner, and Easy Goer, like Alydar, could still make the Hall of Fame.

Sunday Silence stalked a longshot leader and the crowd roared as he made his bid turning for home. Easy Goer was moving with him and then, in a single glorious moment, shot past him and began drawing away to what would be an eight-length victory and the second-fastest Belmont ever behind Secretariat's.

Marshall Cassidy, New York's race caller and the descendant of a family long connected to racing officialdom and The Jockey Club, was known as a clinical and unemotional announcer, but he could not resist editorializing as the wire approached.

"It's *New York's* Easy Goer, in front!"

Marshall lost his announcing job the next year and I always

wondered if his hometown gloat had contributed to his depar-ture. I probably should have been sanctioned myself for the most appallingly unprofessional behavior of my career in a press box. The few remaining Easy Goer loyalists had begun applauding and soon we were pounding each other on the back in glee. I turned to the columnist who had taken a shot at me and snarled, "Creation of the media, huh?!" Only later did I even remember that Easy Goer's victory had completed the pick six and made my ticket worth $34,000, twice what it would have paid had Sunday Silence won.

Of course, I had used both of them on my ticket. Loyalty and vindication are sweet, but in the pick six you just don't throw out one of only two horses who can possibly win a race.

Easy Goer swept the Whitney, Travers, Woodward, and Jockey Club Gold Cup after that and was heavily favored when he next met Sunday Silence, in the 1989 Breeders' Cup Classic at Gulfstream. Sunday Silence got the jump on him again and Easy Goer fell a desperate neck short after a poor start and a debatable ride.

It was a hard loss to take, but was not as depressing as the Belmont had been exhilarating. Sunday Silence had won three of four meetings and even I had to vote for him as the Horse of the Year, but in the final Triple Crown race of a decade that had seen New York displaced as the center of the racing uni-verse, New York's Easy Goer had provided a throwback moment of glory.

EASY GOER'S SUMMER of triumph had also provided me with welcome relief from my first real problem with the *Times* since I had inadvertently offended Abe Rosenthal and delayed my start as the racing writer eight years earlier.

Early that spring, *Sports Illustrated* had decided to do a feature story on Beyer and me, the two slightly disheveled, Harvard-educated racing writers for the nation's two toniest newspapers. The article was entirely lighthearted and flattering, and as always, we freely discussed our gambling. A photographer came to take some pictures of us at the track, and we rejected one suggestion after another for hokey posed shots. He wanted us on horseback. He wanted us to put our ears to the racetrack as if listening for the distant thunder of buffalo. Finally I agreed to stand behind a mutuel window fanning out a handful of hundred-dollar bills.

A week after the piece ran, I was summoned to the office of Max Frankel, who had been Charlotte Curtis's boss back in the op-ed days and had now succeeded Rosenthal as the executive editor of the paper. I thought perhaps I was getting a raise or a personal thanks for representing the paper so well in the *SI* article, but instead he told me we had a serious issue to discuss.

An editor on the financial page had come to him, outraged about the piece. The *Times*'s financial reporters were allowed to own stock but not to dive in and out of the market on companies they wrote about. So why was the racing writer allowed to bet on races he covered?

I explained to Frankel that I saw no parallel. My participation at the windows drove me to pay far more attention to the sport, and the readers benefited from it. Handicapping was like bridge or chess, and I assumed that the *Times*'s bridge and chess columnists were good enough to play in tournaments for cash prizes.

Besides, I mostly wrote about races after they had been run. When I previewed races or made selections, I could in theory only be hurting my price by writing about who I thought might be a good bet, not that I thought *The New York*

Times was having any effect on a single tote board in America. The only way I could profit from my opinions would be if he were suggesting that I could be so corrupt that I was deliberately disseminating disinformation.

That wasn't it, he said. The concern was that because I had access to the stable area and the jockeys' room, I could be receiving "inside information" in advance about who was going to win the races. I tried not to laugh as I relayed the story of how the great jockey Eddie Arcaro had said the job he most wanted upon retirement was to be the bookmaker in the jockeys' room, because riders were such poor handicappers. I tried to explain that my rider and trainer friends asked me which horses I liked, not the other way around.

Frankel was sympathetic but unconvinced, and he and I have different memories of how the situation was resolved. Fourteen years later, he told a fact-checker for *The New Yorker* magazine, which resurrected the incident after the *Times* published a 136-page code of ethics specifically prohibiting racing writers and even editors from any participation in the parimutuel arts, that he thought I had agreed to stop betting. As I remember it, the issue was simply dropped and my boss, Joe Vecchione, correctly told me to stop doing stupid things like posing for pictures with a fistful of dollars.

The *Times* never addressed the matter with me again, but for the first time I was feeling sour about what I had considered the best and luckiest job in the world. Two subsequent episodes furthered my disenchantment.

The *Times* decreed early in 1990 that its reporters could no longer vote for any type of awards, be they for the best film of the year, most valuable player, or champion 2-year-old filly. "We should be above and apart from it," said the memo. "Where we have strong feelings about the quality of various performers, the place to assert those feelings is in the *Times*—where the judgment is not diluted by the votes of others."

By that reasoning, why not also let the Sulzbergers pick the president of the United States rather than having the *Times*'s judgment "diluted by the votes of others"? I was supposed to sit in the corner of the press box in a clerical collar, the only racing writer in the country not allowed to vote for Eclipse Awards or visit the betting windows, simply because I worked for a newspaper that took itself way too seriously.

The *Times*'s wave of self-righteousness was especially hard to accept because the paper was simultaneously adding various silly new sections, pretending that consumer whims in clothing, home decorating, and restaurant openings were serious news in order to attract advertisers. The previous spring, on the afternoon before the Derby, I received a phone call in the Churchill Downs press box telling me to stop whatever I was doing to go track down some information for the "Food" section on the history and lore of mint juleps, including a local recipe.

That summer, I had my first truly bad experience with how one of my stories was edited and presented. This kind of thing probably happened frequently to writers covering national and foreign affairs, whose pieces were filtered through a platoon of editors who used to cover those beats and considered themselves more knowledgeable than the writers. I had always enjoyed the equivalent of being the foreign correspondent to Pluto; my little corner of the universe was obscure and unknown, and my judgment on what was or wasn't a legitimate story was usually accepted.

That year, though, a new editor with limited understanding of racing assigned me a piece on steroid use in Thoroughbreds. A personal friend of his who had a small breeding operation had told him that horses were coming off the racetrack with steroids practically leaking from their nostrils and were unable to breed. It was a provocative premise, but I could find no one but the editor's friend to support it. In weeks of interviews with breeders, both on and off the record, I heard plenty of concern about Lasix and synthetic performance-enhancers, but nothing about steroids. I wrote and submitted a story focusing on those issues, raising and dismissing the subject of steroids.

The editor did not let the facts stand in the way of his agenda and sold it to page 1 of the newspaper on his original premise. An altered version of what I had written was published.

I had thought I would work at the *Times* forever. Now, after 12 years with the company, I was beginning to give serious consideration to the British fellow in a rumpled white suit who had approached me a few months earlier with what seemed like a preposterous idea: to launch a competitor to *Daily Racing Form*.

SUBSTANCE OVER FORM

THE BETTING DISPUTE with the *Times* had radicalized my feelings about the role of wagering in racing. I once had seen them as entirely separate things. Racing was a sport, and there just so happened to be legal gambling on it off to the side.

In fact, they have always been interdependent. The track's cut of the betting pool was what paid the race purses, whether $5,000 for the cheapest claimers or $500,000 for a major stakes. Those race purses were what paid trainers and jockeys and what made owners buy horses. Those horse purchases were what paid breeders to arrange matings and raise foals. Everything came back to the betting dollars, yet the people putting up those dollars were at the bottom of the heap and were generally treated poorly.

Bettors nationwide, for example, had shown a clear preference for multiple bets such as the exacta and trifecta instead of being limited to the old win, place, and show wagers on individual horses. Most tracks, however, doled out these opportunities stingily. The worst offender was Santa Anita, which tried to discourage its customers, or at least those with moderate means, from playing exactas by making the minimum bet $5 rather than the customary $2.

A trade group asked me to debate the issue with Cliff Goodrich, Santa Anita's president, at a convention in Florida in March of 1990. Goodrich said he wanted to "save the customers from themselves" because exactas were riskier bets they would cash less often. This was a common argument at the time, but one that ignored how people actually bet. The horseplayer of yesteryear who spent $6 by betting $2 "across the board" on a horse—$2 to win, place, and show—wasn't going to punch out a single $6 exacta now. What that player wanted was a $1 minimum bet so he could make a three-horse exacta box for $6.

After the debate, an energetic man with a Beatles haircut came bounding up and introduced himself as George White of England's Mirror Group Newspapers. He got right to the point. He wanted to offer me a job to edit a new horse-racing newspaper that would compete with the *Daily Racing Form*.

I told him I was flattered but that taking on the *Form* was an impossible dream. Founded as a four-page daily in 1894, the *Form* had enjoyed a virtual monopoly on the racing data needed to produce past performances. It had been owned for most of its history by the Annenberg family, which had made its initial fortune by cornering the market on telegraph transmissions of race results. The *Form,* with a similar stranglehold on data, had become one of the great cash cows of American business, the cornerstone of a publishing empire that later included *TV Guide* and *Seventeen* magazine.

The *Form* had been an embedded part of the industry for nearly a century and had crushed the few competitive startups over the years by leveraging its racetrack relationships. Only one outfit had made a serious run at it: *Sports Eye,* which published past performances for harness racing, had twice expanded into Thoroughbred past performances. Both times the *Form* had threatened tracks with nondelivery of the paper if they allowed *Sports Eye* employees to call charts from the press box and sold the product at the track.

These tactics only went so far, though, and the *Form* eventually had to reach private "settlements" to keep *Sports Eye* from continuing to publish. It was unclear whether *Sports Eye's* true goal had been to establish a real business or just to be paid for discontinuing one, but either way, it had profited from its attempts.

More recently, in 1989, a bizarre paper named *F.I.G.S. Form* had imploded before posing enough of a threat to merit a settlement. Backed by a stubborn eccentric named Robert Sinn, *F.I.G.S. Form* had presented past performances as a sort of hybrid between conventional running lines and Ragozin Sheets-style graphics, and ended up looking like the schematic diagram for a vacuum cleaner. It had been a bad product and vanished quickly when its funds ran out after a few months.

I recounted this history to White and told him to save his breath. While improving journalistically on the stodgy and cheerleading *Form* was a noble goal, only a madman with money to burn could even think about taking on the *Form* in the marketplace.

As it turned out, White represented exactly such an individual: Robert Maxwell, a British media tycoon, whose holdings included book publishers, British tabloids, and *The Sporting Life,* England's equivalent of the *Form.* Maxwell had seen a deep-pocketed startup called *The Racing Post* take 30 percent of the *Life's* business away in England, and thought the same could be done to the *Form* stateside.

Maxwell had another burning interest in the *Form.* Two years earlier, it had been sold by Walter Annenberg's Triangle Publications to Rupert Murdoch, the Australian publishing magnate whom Maxwell saw as his global rival. White said Maxwell enjoyed nothing more than jousting with Murdoch and was prepared to spend whatever it took to devalue the *Form.*

That made the whole idea intriguing, but I was unconvinced that even Maxwell could do it, and White left Florida with nothing more than my best wishes. Over the next few months, though, the idea began to take hold in my mind.

Outside of Joe Hirsch and a few of its handicappers, the *Form* was a pretty sorry excuse for a newspaper, both editorially and statistically. The writing was uninspired and formulaic, controversial matters were rarely even addressed, and the wagering public that bought almost all the copies was largely ignored. Instead, every racing celebrity was routinely hailed as a delightful individual or a visionary manager.

The first mention of every horse's name in a news story was preceded by his owner's name—Dr. Carter was "Mrs. Frances A. Genter's Dr. Carter," giving the stories the feeling of a fawning dog-show program meant to flatter owners rather than a sports newspaper written for the customers. What sports page would ever begin a story about a baseball game by writing that "Mr. George Steinbrenner's New York Yankees yesterday defeated Mr. Peter Angelos's Baltimore Orioles by a score of 7 to 2"?

The *Form* also functioned as three entirely separate companies, with offices near New York, Chicago, and Los Angeles. News coverage was regionalized to save pages, so New Yorkers read stories and columns about second-tier racing in Boston, Philadelphia, and Baltimore when they wanted to know about major racing in Kentucky or California.

Even the past performances, the industry standard everyone used, were seeming increasingly inadequate. Granted, I took things more seriously than most *Form* users, but I was spending up to four hours a night marking up my past performances with additional information that the *Form* simply chose not to provide. The biggest task was calculating and entering my own speed figures into the paper, but there were plenty of other monastic chores I had to undertake—looking up horses' pedigrees and produce records, manually compiling their histories at different tracks and surfaces, and hunting through piles of yellowing newspapers to find information that was no longer in the *Form's* 10 most recent running lines for each horse.

White approached me again in April to say he thought the fundamental data issue in launching a startup could be solved. Maxwell had met with Dinny Phipps of The Jockey Club and proposed paying to accelerate something the racing industry was already starting to do: compile its own database.

In the Annenberg days, the *Form* had never missed an edition, which would have left the public without past performances to bet with, but now industry leaders were concerned what might happen under Murdoch. What if a labor strike at his other properties spread to the *Form*? Shouldn't the industry own the records of its own races, if only as a backup?

The barrier was cost. Employing people to collect data at every track in the country would require at least $2 million a year. Maxwell proposed a solution: He would help fund this new collection venture, paying $800,000 a year to start, if the industry would give the data to his new racing paper. He became the first client of Equibase, a joint venture of The Jockey Club and the tracks, which began collecting data in 1991. For earlier data, Maxwell had bought the assets of *F.I.G.S. Form*, which had a choppy database going back to 1988.

I told White it sounded as if he now had a shot but that I still needed more proof of Maxwell's commitment to the project. Maxwell responded that White should bring me to England to meet him and to see his operation, and to prove his largesse he would fly me over first class and then back home on the Concorde. I toured Maxwell's newsrooms and was duly impressed, especially by *The Sporting Life*. The paper was made up in full color and on computer screens, a new development that hadn't reached United States newspapers.

Maxwell greeted me in a boardroom. He was an enormous man with a thundering voice, huge eyebrows, and hair dyed jet black. He welcomed me to his employ, seemingly under the impression that I had already agreed to come aboard. We had a completely confusing conversation and I finally had to tell him I couldn't even think about joining his enterprise without a serious long-term offer. He told me to enjoy the ride home on the Concorde and to meet him in New York in two weeks.

White and I spent an afternoon at Ascot racecourse and the evening betting on greyhounds at Wembley Stadium with Katherine Wilkins, a colleague of White's who he said would be the marketing director for the new project. The next morning we went to the country estate of one of Maxwell's sons and ate blood pudding in front of a huge picture window looking onto a meadow full of sheep. If nothing else, I had gotten a free whirlwind weekend in England out of the whole proposition.

I arrived at Maxwell's New York hotel 14 days later and took a private elevator to a rooftop suite of rooms. The waiting area had half a dozen fax machines constantly spitting out paper, and every available surface was covered with enormous, half-eaten platters of Chinese food. People were yelling into telephones in other rooms, and there was constant traffic in and out of the back part of the suite where Maxwell was staying, including arrivals and departures by exotic-looking women. Had there been a mime, the scene could have passed for an outtake from a Fellini film.

Maxwell finally emerged from the back bedroom and ushered me out onto the rooftop. It was one of those perfect summer days when you could see for miles from the center of New York, and Maxwell repeatedly swung his meaty arms at the city below as he made his pitch in a booming voice.

"Never forget this day, my boy," he said. "Today is your day of destiny. The city shall be yours. You shall invent the greatest racing newspaper the world has ever seen and I shall make you a millionaire and many more millions for myself. What are you paid now?"

"Sixty thousand," I said, exaggerating by only 20 percent.

"I'll start you at seventy-five," he said, "and we'll have you up to a hundred in a year."

He was gone a minute later, saying I would be hearing from his people, but over the next three months little happened. White came up to Saratoga with Katherine, and everyone acted as if we were already in business together, but I still had no offer.

Time was on my side. I had a great job despite my mixed feelings about the *Times*. Word had begun to circulate that

Maxwell was undertaking a racing newspaper the following spring, so he would have to name the editor soon. I would never again be in such a good bargaining position. My lawyer and business adviser, an old acquaintance named Bruce Margolius, counseled me to wait them out and he rejected one offer after another, all of them based on a $75,000 starting salary and participation in various complicated long-term equity and bonus schemes that Bruce didn't trust.

Finally, in October, Bruce told Maxwell's people to forget about everything except Maxwell's promise to make me a millionaire, and that we wanted that to happen in five years rather than 13 and strictly through a fat salary that would grow fatter each year. To our amazement, they agreed, producing a contract on the day before the 1990 Breeders' Cup.

I didn't sign it immediately. The whole prospect still seemed daunting, as did giving up a job I had always called the best in the world. I got paid to go to the track, and to winter in Florida and summer in Saratoga. Still, the possibilities of the new venture were uniquely tempting: creating a daily racing paper people would actually want to read, improving the past performances, addressing the customers' concerns. How many journalists ever get to invent a whole new newspaper?

I covered the Breeders' Cup races Saturday and on Sunday wrote what I was pretty sure would be my final *Times* column, ending it with the word *farewell* as a private flourish. The next day was my 34th birthday and I went into the *Times* to tell them I was leaving. It was a new sports editor's first day on the job, and he thought I was making a play for a raise. When I told him that Maxwell would be tripling my *Times* salary, he said that was a lot more than he was being paid and I should probably take it.

He called downstairs to inform the higher-ups that I was leaving, and came back to me with a final offer to stay, a sort of perfect misunderstanding of me that made leaving all the easier: How would I like to be a Washington correspondent? I shook everyone's hands, then went home and signed the Maxwell contract.

We scheduled a press conference about the new venture in the Aqueduct press box later that week, and White said we had to decide on a name for it by then. It came to me in an instant, and I later heard it annoyed more than flattered my former employer.

"There's only one candidate," I said. "Let's call it *The Racing Times*."

TWO DAYS LATER I reported to my new career at an address on Spring Street in lower Manhattan. The front door was broken and a hand-lettered sign directed me up a flight of rickety stairs to a door with two more signs: "*The Racing Times*," clipped from the press release, and a larger official notice reading "Danger—Rat Poison." I briefly wondered how much of a pay cut I might have to take to get my job back at the other *Times*.

It didn't get much better inside, where the five or six other employees of the new venture were isolated in corners of a large single room with a few battered desks and bookcases. This was what was left of *F.I.G.S. Form*, the short-lived start-up that Maxwell had purchased to get some old data. White cheerfully welcomed me aboard, assured me we would be moving to state-of-the-art offices soon, and we spent the day talking about how we would take on the 96-year-old, 400-man *Daily Racing Form*.

It was a mammoth undertaking and we didn't have much time. Maxwell had personally decreed that the paper start publishing by April 1 to begin recouping the $20 million he was investing. So we had five months to recruit and hire a staff, set up offices in the Midwest and California, install a new desktop-publishing system that had never been used in North America, and reinvent racing journalism and statistics along the way.

What had I gotten myself into?

To me, the editorial part would be the easiest, because it was largely a matter of hiring the right people. I knew the talented writers and sharpest handicappers in most markets from a decade in press boxes and from reading the freelancers in the weeklies. I wanted a separate reporter and handicapper in each major circuit and a one-man team in smaller markets.

In all its years, the *Form* had never gone out and hired a well-known writer and did not even identify most of its handicappers, relying instead on an overworked desk of proofreaders who made picks under fictitious names such as Hermis or Sweep. The public assumed these were individuals' pen names, but in fact Hermis on Thursday was not the same Hermis as on Friday or Saturday. How were readers supposed to know whom to follow?

Fortunately, many of my top candidates wanted to be part of the new enterprise. They too had spent years relying on the *Form* as a unique information source while lamenting its shortcomings, and Maxwell seemed to be the first person with a real chance to establish an alternative. It also was a time when many newspapers were cutting back on their section sizes in general and their racing coverage in particular, leaving top racing writers concerned about their futures and especially willing to jump ship.

I was able to recruit most of my wish list, which included Dale Austin, Clem Florio, and Jack Mann from Baltimore and

Washington; Steve Davidowitz; Brad Free from *The National*; Art Grace from the *Miami News*; Jay Hovdey from California; Kurt Paseka from New York's *Daily News*; Chuck Streva in Florida; Mike Watchmaker from the *Form*; and Jack Will in Kentucky. Others agreed to contribute columns for the daily op-ed and handicapping-forum pages I was planning, including Neil Campbell in Toronto, Russ Harris and Bill Finley from the *Daily News*, Kent Hollingsworth from *The Blood-Horse*, Dick Jerardi from *The Philadelphia Daily News*, Bill Leggett from *Sports Illustrated*, Michael Veitch of *The Saratogian*, and the authors William Murray and James Quinn.

The new paper was an opportunity for other people who knew racing to try something different. Steve Schwartz, the New York Racing Association's director of media relations most of the time I had worked in the press box, wanted to switch sides and became our New Jersey reporter. Karen Johnson and Steve Schuelein made similar transitions in New York and California. John Pricci, the handicapper for Long Island's *Newsday*, had become nearly as interested in basketball and football and signed on as a sports-betting columnist.

For some other writers, the startup was a chance to move inside and become editors and managers. For our two main bureaus outside New York, I got Jay Privman from the *Daily News* of Los Angeles to head up the California office and Ray Paulick from *The Thoroughbred Times* to run the Midwest operation, which we would locate in Lexington, Kentucky, instead of Chicago.

For top editorial deputies in New York, I had Irwin Cohen, who had worked for *Sports Eye* and its weekly *Racing Action* magazine; Neil Cook from *The Sporting Life* to install the new production system and put the paper out mechanically; and Rob Schneider, who had worked for NYRA and The Jockey

Club. For the chief copy editor, I turned to the best one I knew and hired Robin.

Rich Rosenbush was the only *New York Times* employee I tried to steal away, but after agonizing over it for a while he said no. Later, though, I got a call from Evan Jenkins, a key *Times* newsroom editor and racing fan who was taking early retirement but thought he had a thing or two to teach young journalists. Could we use a seasoned newsroom hand? Chuck Slater, a veteran editor who had run the sports department of the *Daily News,* also liked the idea of working with some youngsters on a startup and completed the editorial team.

For copy editors, we put ads in a few small local papers and got a tremendous response. Robin devised an editing test where we gave applicants a story written in the worst possible *Daily Racing Form* jargon and asked them to correct it. (They got extra credit if they had the good instinct to delete a gratuitous quotation from the winning trainer saying that "I'd like to take this opportunity to thank the wonderful owners for having contributed so much to the sport of racing," a gracious sentiment but one that has no place in a news story.)

We awarded jobs to the highest scorers and ended up with a wonderfully eclectic desk that included Victor Mather, a math wiz who was editing crossword puzzles; Lauren Stich, a pedigree enthusiast who had worked at the *Form* 20 years earlier before going on to sing professionally; David McDonough, whom I hadn't seen in the 17 years since he had edited my school newspaper, the *Trinity Times,* a year after I graduated; and Duke Dosik, a *Sports Eye* editor I had met in a weekly poker game.

All of them knew and liked the game and wanted to be part of the new paper. If anything, I had underestimated how many people shared my dissatisfaction with the *Form*. As word of the venture spread, racing fans began writing and showing up at our offices offering to do anything to help.

I got a letter from a reclusive bookstore employee, Alan Shuback, who had devoted himself to the full-time hobby of creating running lines for top European races by reading foreign accounts and watching imported videotapes. He offered to create past performances for foreign runners this way, a vast improvement over the *Form*'s dismissively sketchy foreign running lines at the time.

I knew that the biggest statistical innovation *The Racing Times* would offer would be real speed figures. I toyed briefly with training people to make them the way I did, and White lobbied for those made by Jerry Brown's Thorograph, an offshoot of Ragozin's The Sheets. The clear choice, though, was to go with the person whose name was synonymous with the figs.

Two years earlier, Beyer had begun selling his figures to a small audience of pioneering personal-computer users through a company called Bloodstock Research Information Services, and had formed a group including Joe Cardello and Mark Hopkins from the original Florida pick-six team to produce figures for all the major tracks. Fortunately, his Bloodstock Research deal was short-term and Maxwell agreed to a much more generous arrangement. By February, we could announce that *The Racing Times* would feature Beyer Speed Figures in the past-performance lines.

So we had Davidowitz on staff and Beyer's figures. I completed the trifecta of the first three handicappers I had come to admire by seeking out Tom Ainslie, who had never been asked to write by the *Form* or any newspaper despite having singlehandedly promoted intelligent handicapping for so long.

Ainslie agreed not only to contribute a weekly column but also to write a one-page explanation of the new *Racing Times* past performances that would appear in the paper every day.

I knew there were many other elements besides speed figures I wanted to introduce into the past performances, and I was getting legal advice to make as many changes as possible with both new data and the presentation of the traditional elements. We were fully expecting the *Form* to try to restrain our publication just before launch by claiming that we were violating their copyright on past performances. It was the opinion of Maxwell's lawyers, however, that the past performances themselves could not be copyrighted—almost every one of the dozens of pieces of information in each running line was public information. The only proprietary data were the chart callers' comments and estimations of the margins separating each horse at intermediate points of call, and we would be getting our own such information through Equibase.

The attorneys believed, however, that there was a potential copyright challenge on the arrangement and presentation of all the data if it looked too much like a *Form*. I didn't agree with them—harness and greyhound racing used a very similar presentation in track-produced programs, and there were only a few logical ways to arrange the numbers. Still, the attorneys insisted that we make some arbitrary changes along with my planned improvements to withstand a copyright suit.

For example, the *Form* listed a horse's post position at the left of the running line, and the number of horses who had run in the race at the far right. So it seemed both more logical, and something that would please the lawyers, to move the two figures next to each other. Instead of seeing a "2" many columns to the left of a "9," *The Racing Times* would put them together as "⅔"—meaning a horse had started from post 2 in a field of nine.

I used my own marked-up *Form*s as the template for additional information. I had always hand-drawn a line between past-performance lines if the races had been more than 90 days apart. This became the "layoff line," automatically inserted between widely spaced races.

I asked every writer and handicapper to propose new elements. There were marathon meetings and conference calls, usually deadlocked between traditionalists such as Ainslie and Davidowitz, who urged restraint, and a more radical wing that said now was the time to change as much as possible. I usually came down somewhere in the middle, adding the most useful new features while trying to keep it looking more like a *Daily Racing Form* than a *F.I.G.S. Form*.

When horses made their debuts, the *Form* printed only their four most recent workouts, and handicappers would have to pore through weeks of workout listings to find previous ones. So we went to two lines of workouts, up to a total of eight.

The *Form* told you a horse's current-year and previous-year records, but what about his performances at various distances and surfaces? We created the "career box," showing each horse's record for the current and previous year, and lifetime statistics for wet tracks, grass courses, and races at today's track and distance.

The *Form* had an ancient practice of presenting a horse's pedigree by listing the sire, the dam, and the dam's sire. But what about the sire's sire? Every year there were new stallions, some of them unraced, or at least unfamiliar to most racing fans. If a 2-year-old by an unknown sire named Obligato appeared in the entries, wasn't it helpful to know that Obligato was by Northern Dancer? So we added the sire's sire to the data field as well as the horse's month of birth, so readers would know that a Pleasant Colony had been a late foal.

We made many other small improvements and three final big ones.

The first was to add a second line to each of a horse's last three past performances to accommodate a lengthy "trip note" on what had happened to him during the race. The *Form's* lines allowed for just a dozen or so characters at the end of the line, room enough only for a usually worthless one- or two-word digest of information obvious from the data: "Late rally" or "Led, stopped." Under the direction of our field supervisor, Richard McCarthy, we hired skilled racewatchers at the major tracks, such as Paul Cornman in New York, to compose a 50-character description of relevant additional information.

The second was to change the lineup of tracks in each edition. The *Form* had always printed thoroughly regional editions, so a New Yorker would buy a paper with past performances for New York, Boston, New Jersey, and Pennsylvania—not because New Yorkers were interested in those tracks, but because the *Form* could print one edition for those four areas. Instead we included the major tracks around the country that were of more interest to horsemen, owners, and fans. A New York edition might include the races from Florida, Kentucky, and California instead of just the second-tier tracks in the Northeast.

The third was of little interest to most horseplayers but something I felt strongly about: reporting times in hundredths rather than fifths of a second. For years, tracks had been using equipment that gave the times that precisely, but only New York reported them that way, and even there you had to be at the track to copy them down.

The *Form* had continued to print times only in fifths, a practice I considered a symbol of the sport's and that paper's sloppiness when it came to information. Every other timed sport, such as swimming or track and field, used hundredths, yet racing, where people were betting millions a day, used fifths because that's how old-time stopwatches were calibrated. (The only newspaper in the country that printed the times in hundredths was, of all places, *The New York Times,* in its tiny agate results. In my final year there, Rich Rosenbush had pushed the editors to make the change, and it was a clerk's job each day to call the track and get the precise times.)

To my mind, using fifths of a second introduced an unacceptable degree of rounding and vagueness into the game's key measuring stick. Two consecutive six-furlong races on the same card might be run in 1:11.00 and 1:11.19, but both races would be reported as having been run in 1:11 flat. That difference of nineteen hundredths of a second amounts to more than a length—which translated to 1.8 points on my speed figures (three full points on the modern Beyer scale)—but was being routinely buried by the *Form* and was unavailable to anyone but a New York handicapper copying things down off the track's television monitors.

The problem could be doubled when you were trying to figure out an internal fraction. Suppose you were attempting to compare the come-home times of two Derby prospects in separate one-mile races. Both races might have posted times of 1:12 and 1:37, suggesting that both had a final quarter of 25 seconds. What if the true times of these events were as follows:

| Race A | 1:12.00 | 1:37.19 |
| Race B | 1:12.19 | 1:37.00 |

Now we can see that the come-home time was actually 25.19 seconds in Race A, and a significantly faster 24.81 seconds in Race B. People understandably think hundredths of a second are so tiny as to be insignificant, but 38 of them, the difference in the example above, amount to 2¼ lengths.

Beyer Speed Figures, extended trip notes, times in hundredths, career boxes, sires' sires, layoff lines, past performances from all the top tracks, and an all-star lineup of writers and handicappers. How could *The Racing Times* miss?

WHITE DELIVERED ON his promise of the new offices. Late in 1990, we moved a few blocks west to the top floor at 315 Hudson Street. There was brand-new equipment in the center of the massive room for the writers, editors, and production people, and new offices ringing the floor for the editorial and business executives.

The new space lifted everyone's spirits, but the challenge of getting a paper launched by April still appeared impossible, and the business people seemed particularly low. They didn't really get what the editorial types were up to and why this paper should do any better than *Sports Eye* or *F.I.G.S. Form* before it.

I was too busy to be betting seriously and had even stopped making my own figures, ending a daily ritual that had gone uninterrupted since 1983. But one day there was a two-day pick-six carryover at Aqueduct and I decided to play it using the first pass of Beyer Speed Figures we now had in our system. I went door to door in the office selling 1 percent shares in a $600 play to the business folks, who didn't fully understand why I wanted $6 from them. Their faith in the entire *Racing Times* enterprise seemed renewed when I hit for $51,000 and handed them each a tax-adjusted $365 at the end of the day.

(When I went to cash the winning ticket at the nearby OTB, the tellers looked at it as if it were a radioactive meteorite and said they didn't keep that kind of cash around and could only offer me 18 checks for $2,000 because all their checks were stamped "Not valid if over $2,000.")

The winning shareholders included our technology wizards, who until then had really not understood that there was a connection between the real world and the systems they were feverishly building. We had lucked into a world-class technology chief in Aman Safaei, who had run the highest level of computer systems for the shah of Iran before being forced to flee the country and answer a classified ad for a new horse-racing newspaper.

Neither he nor the largely immigrant group of programmers and developers he recruited had ever seen a horse race, and the learning curve was daunting. Irwin and I had a lengthy argument with a programmer who insisted that he could not accommodate dead heats in the database because "two horses cannot occupy same space at same time." Somehow, participating in the office pick six seemed to clarify these and other issues, and several programmers became betting fanatics.

Aman's systems worked wonderfully and we were looking at dazzling past-performance prototypes well before the launch. Our biggest problem was populating the database with enough race calls to generate meaningful past performances. Equibase had been collecting data for less than a year, and there were plenty of holes in the *F.I.G.S. Form* information. Also, everything had to be manually keyed in, and we had to set up a 30-person sweatshop of temps who typed in data around the clock. Two weeks before the launch, we discovered four months of results from one circuit that had never been entered and were sitting in a box under someone's desk.

The *Form*'s response to impending competition was curious. It didn't hire a single writer or handicapper or introduce any new features to the paper. Instead, it announced a new offer to supply the tracks with a few scraps of past-performance data to include in track programs, believing this generous gesture would cement its relationships with the tracks and discourage them from selling *The Racing Times*.

The proposal was too little too late. The prospect of a serious alternative to the *Form*, with profits perhaps eventually flowing back to the tracks through their ownership of Equibase, had awakened many track operators to just how poorly they really had been treated by the *Form* for decades. The paper could be counted on to come out every day and to say nice things about everyone in the business, but the tracks made only pennies on each sale and were forced to take the paper with a unique no-returns policy for unsold copies.

The *Form* as a company had been a highly profitable printing operation that did no advertising and promotion. Maxwell's personal and professional style was to make a splash wherever he went. As White and Katherine Wilkins visited tracks in the weeks before our launch, they learned that no one from the *Form* had ever worked with the tracks' marketing departments to sponsor and create events such as giveaways and handicapping seminars. There was a huge opportunity there for a well-funded startup, and even before the launch there were *Racing Times* caps, pens, and tote bags all over the tracks.

The *Form* had never run a television commercial, but we shot several. For two days in February, a Hollywood crew armed with smoke machines and fresh paint invaded the newsroom and filmed a slick spot promising "real speed figures, real trip notes, and the best writers and handicappers in the business." Racing celebrities including Angel Cordero Jr. and Charlie Whittingham were featured, and I delivered the kicker, a variation of the "Substance over Form" slogan that Irwin Cohen had come up with.

"Either you're a paper of substance," I sternly told the camera, "or you're just a *Form.*"

The data needed another two months, but we were locked into an April launch, especially after Maxwell threw a lavish party at the Rainbow Room in Manhattan on April 3 that attracted not only racing's poobahs but dignitaries from publishing and politics and even an official from the Archdiocese of New York, who must not have been informed that this was a newspaper for gamblers. I sat between Maxwell and Mayor David Dinkins and we all made speeches.

Maxwell had no interest in the details of the operation except to insist on a few personal preferences. He wanted the front page of the paper to be printed in full color to distinguish it from the *Form,* which used a single red box around its logo and was otherwise entirely black-and-white. He asked for more than a dozen revisions of the logo, but when we told him we were missing important historical racing data, he simply suggested we "copy it out of the *Form* and jumble it up a little so we don't get sued."

The week before the launch was a sleepless marathon. The first time we tried to send a full-color front page to the printer over the phone lines, it took 14 hours to go through. The past performances looked great despite too many blank spaces in the bottom of each horse's set of running lines where we didn't have any internal points of call.

Ready or not, the first *Racing Times* rolled off the presses for the racing of Saturday, April 13, 1991. There were eight pages of news, opinion columns, and handicapping articles as opposed to the *Form*'s usual four pages of editorial in front of the past performances. The front page was in glorious color and crammed with race-at-a-glance charts and photographs. It was a debut everyone was proud of, and the paper would only get bigger and better with time.

It was hard to tell how we were doing in the marketplace. We gave the paper away for a week, and once we started charging for it, sales figures were as erratic as our hastily constructed distribution network. Maxwell's clout through his other publications got us carried on big-city newsstands, but we hadn't had time to penetrate the unique network of convenience and liquor stores where players had been buying the *Form* every day for years, if not decades.

High-end handicappers loved the new data and fans said they enjoyed having something to read, but we were asking rank-and-file horseplayers to abandon an old and familiar friend and not making it an easy transition. They were ready for a change, but wouldn't make it if they couldn't rely on getting the paper every day.

We hadn't planned on many people using both products, but found that a lot of players were buying both a $2 *Racing Times* and a $3 *Form*. I spotted a few friends at the track using the *Form* and took it as a personal insult. They explained that they loved reading *The Racing Times* but copied the Beyer figures and our other stats into their *Forms* because they were just too accustomed to the look of the traditional product. We found we were doing much better with newer and younger customers than with ones who had been playing the game with the same tool for decades.

I agonized over revamping the look of the past performances. The lawyers had been wrong about a copyright-infringement lawsuit from the *Form,* and clearly we had gone too far in altering the look of the running lines. Readers liked the additional information, but we had probably made too many changes, and all at once. A handful of time junkies loved the hundredths, but more readers missed the old convenience and look of fifths. In retrospect, we should have just put them in the results charts for those who wanted them, instead of trying to convert everyone to a metric system overnight.

The data gaps were another barrier to potential converts, and several racing writers criticized us sharply for them, grudgingly conceding that our product was superior but warning readers about the reliability of the data, scaring them away. I was stung by the unexpectedly cool reaction from the racing press, but shouldn't have been. It had never occurred to me that every time I had said in an interview or press release that *The Racing Times* had assembled all of the nation's best writers and handicappers, I was unintentionally insulting anyone I hadn't asked to join the team.

The *Form* noted our existence only to point out missing lines in an unnamed competitive product. Bill Dow, then a general manager and later the president of the *Form*, told me years later how he and the company had reacted to the new paper.

"I was sick to my stomach when I looked at the first issue of *The Racing Times*," he said, "because I knew that editorially it was better than anything we could do. We couldn't compete with it. But when I looked at the data problems, I knew we had some time for Maxwell to self-destruct or run out of money."

Still, as the early weeks passed, we were making progress in the market and having a lot of fun in print. Despite running news meetings and having new business and promotional duties, I was writing regularly for the paper and even making selections for big races. Our reporters and columnists were writing about racing in a way the *Form* never had, addressing the needs and issues of horseplayers first. Unlike the *Form*, where every horse was afforded a sporting chance and selectors were anonymous, our bylined handicappers dispensed opinions and betting advice.

On the day of the Coaching Club American Oaks, a showdown between the charismatic fillies Meadow Star and Lite Light, our front page was dominated by two spirited and opposing handicapping analyses by Kurt Paseka and Mike Watchmaker. When Lite Light romped and her owner, the flamboyant rapper MC Hammer, came to the press box for a news conference, the first thing he did was demand to talk to Paseka, to give him some good-natured abuse for picking against her.

Kurt prompted a memorable front page at Saratoga that summer when he so disliked a chronic runner-up named El Senor that he wrote that if the horse won, he would "dance naked in the Saratoga infield." Naturally, El Senor won. Always one to honor his wagers, Kurt gamely posed in the infield for a front-page photograph, apparently wearing only a strategically positioned *Racing Times*.

Being the editor in chief of a paper instead of just a reporter and columnist had not been as big a transition as I had expected. Recruiting and hiring people was actually fun, and managing a news-gathering operation required journalistic common sense rather than business-school training. The only startling thing was learning that in the eyes of the outside world, everything in the paper was now my doing or my fault whether or not I had written it.

Track operators were not accustomed to seeing questions and criticisms about how they ran their businesses and treated their customers, and early on I received several sputtering calls from officials saying that the *Form* had never subjected them to any scrutiny and who were we to do things differently? One of our writers, Tim Thornton, was actually barred from the Suffolk Downs press box in the middle of the winter simply for reporting a police matter that was in the public record, and had to work out of the icy grandstand.

Maxwell was becoming both more famous and more peculiar than ever. He had bought New York's *Daily News* with a vague idea of transforming it into a British-style tabloid but was losing buckets of money. George White was growing increasingly uncomfortable with Maxwell's business moves and told me one day that huge sums of money had been suddenly showing up in *Racing Times* bank accounts only to disappear a day or two later.

One day Maxwell was in New York and summoned me and White to a lunch where he had clearly been downing wine long before we got there and was amusing himself with a couple of women seated with him at the head of the table. He asked how the paper was doing in California, and White told him progress had been slow.

"Then close the California operation!" he thundered. "I want it closed today!"

I tried explaining that this wasn't the same as shutting down an unprofitable retail outlet in a chain, that there was news and racing in California that was important to the rest of the country, but he barely heard me and dismissed us. Stunned, I asked White how we should proceed.

"Give him a day to sleep it off and he won't even remember it," he said, and fortunately he was right.

ONE MORNING THAT FALL as I was dressing for work, I heard a bulletin on the radio that Robert Maxwell was missing at sea somewhere off the coast of Spain. The employees were worried about what this meant for the paper, but after talking with

White I told them there didn't seem to be any need to panic. We were owned by one of Maxwell's British subsidiaries, Mirror Group, and there was no reason to think it would be anything but business as usual at all the newspapers.

Instead, it was the beginning of the end. As the executors and lawyers began sorting out the Maxwell empire, it started to unravel. There had been wholesale looting of pension funds, and corporate debt was out of control. All but the core properties were put up for sale, and oversight of the American newspapers was given to Charlie Wilson, a senior Mirror executive who soon came to visit.

Wilson was a small and wiry Scotsman with a thick brogue, a sour attitude, and no interest whatsoever in the journalistic or handicapping edification of the American horseplayer. "You're servin' a steak to a fish 'n' chips crowd that would pay the same for a plate of crap," was his assessment of the paper. He said that if he couldn't sell *The Racing Times* pretty quickly, he would simply fire half the staff.

There were a few interested buyers, but one of them was determined to make a quick deal and discourage any other bidders: K-III Holdings, the acquisition arm of the buyout giant Kohlberg Kravis Roberts and Company, which earlier that year had purchased the *Form* from Murdoch for around $250 million. To shut us down and regain its monopoly, the *Form* was willing to top anyone else's bid.

KKR was willing to flex its corporate clout to get it done. The other serious potential buyer was a successful publisher who loved racing and wanted to see *The Racing Times* flourish in its current form. He was willing to do the deal as a break-even for himself just to keep the paper alive. Then he received a phone call from someone at KKR, which also owned major tobacco companies, saying he could forget about ever receiving another dollar in cigarette advertising in his tabloids if he didn't get out of the *Form*'s way.

The walls were closing in. I tried anyone I had ever met who might have access to money. I spent two days in Las Vegas waiting for a promised phone call from a mysterious group of Arab sheikhs who were camped out in the biggest suite at the Mirage hotel. They had started buying horses and were looking at other American investments. They finally paged me, but all they wanted to talk about were the pedigrees of the yearlings they had just bought.

Dinny Phipps was my last hope as a buyer, either on his own or on behalf of The Jockey Club and Equibase. He seemed interested, until he got the prospectus and financials from the broker the Maxwell executives had hired to shop the product. He said that in 25 years of looking at possible acquisitions, he had never seen a presentation so clearly designed to dissuade potential buyers. In his personal opinion, *The Racing Times* was as good as sold to the *Form*, and the sale process was a charade to counter any possible antitrust allegations.

On the afternoon of February 6, 1992, I was writing a column when I looked up from the keyboard to see three unwelcome visitors striding through the front door of *The Racing Times*. I recognized Charlie Wilson but not the two hard-boiled gentlemen behind him. I did notice they had not bothered to button their jackets to conceal the firearms holstered at their belts. Wilson headed straight for my office, while the goons took up posts on either side of the front door.

The rumors of a sale had been strong that afternoon, which is why I had been frantically typing what I thought would be our obituary. If I was right, "Farewell, Readers" was going to be the headline on our final paper that night. Now Wilson was telling me that I had missed the deadline and a sale to the *Form* had been signed.

"But tonight's paper is almost done," I told him. "We're already sending pages to the printer."

"You don't get it," he replied. "You're trespassing."

The troops were gathered for the news that they should shut down their computers, since they too were suddenly unemployed and trespassing. The staff headed for the nearest bar, drank way too much, and toasted to the eternal life of *The Racing Times* and the eternal damnation of the *Daily Racing Form*. The next morning, a lot of hungover trespassers returned to Hudson Street to empty their desks under the supervision of the armed goons, who turned out to be not such bad guys, for armed goons.

"They told us they didn't know how the people here would react," one of them, a retired city police detective, explained when asked why he was packing heat. "But what's someone at a newspaper gonna do, throw a typewriter?" The goons pantomimed checking everyone's bags on the way out, but pretended not to notice all the office supplies, *Racing Times* merchandise, and even a few laptop computers that went out the door that day.

The official version of what happened was not that *The Racing Times* had been sold, but that the Maxwell estate had reached an independent judgment to shut down the property and, just coincidentally, had then sold the shuttered company's assets to the *Form*. This was complete fiction but at least it meant that almost everybody got 90 days' pay under federal law governing plant shutdowns.

The *Form* felt it had scored a victory and was cockier than ever. Equibase, which now had no funding or retail product to sustain itself, met repeatedly with *Form* management and proposed what sounded like a no-lose deal: Why not merge the data-collection operations, saving both companies several million dollars a year, and give the industry co-ownership of the new data but the *Form* an exclusive on using it in full past performances?

The *Form* basically told Equibase to take a long walk off a short pier. It had been around for nearly a century, didn't need partners, and the game couldn't get by without it. If the industry wanted to waste money collecting data, that was its business, but the *Form* would continue to operate as it always had. It was a historic decision that would play itself out in fascinating ways I could never have anticipated.

For now, though, I was simply unemployed and without prospects. *The Racing Times* experience had not made me enthusiastic about working in newspaper management with the Charlie Wilsons of the world. I had burned my bridges to *The New York Times*, and working for the *Form* was unthinkable, not that they wanted me. From the entire editorial operation, only Neil Cook and his page-production team were offered jobs at the *Form*. A few months later the *Form* added color to its front page and the Beyer figures to its past performances, but nothing else about the spirit or content of the paper changed.

After a month of hiding out at home and spending all day on the telephone commiserating with the *Racing Times* crew, it was time to get out of the house and do something. My piano playing was rustier than ever, so I did the only other thing I knew how. I bought a box of spiral-bound graph-paper notebooks and razor-tipped felt pens and began making speed figures for the last three months at Aqueduct so I could start going to the track and playing the pick six again.

TURNING PRO

AT SOME POINT every horseplayer, especially right after a successful day, dreams of making his hobby his job and supporting himself by winning regularly at the track. Few actually attempt it and fewer succeed, but it was time for me to try. Before being office-bound at *The Racing Times* had cut my betting to a recreational trickle, I had been showing an annual profit thanks to the pick six, and I was hopeful I could do even better if I made betting my full-time job.

I holed up at home for a few weeks, getting caught up on recent racing and making figures, then resumed the familiar routine of driving out to the track each day. At first I tried going back to my old seat in the press box, but I left it for good after a week. Looking at other reporters and handicappers covering the game now was a painful reminder of the shutdown of *The Racing Times*. There were empty seats where our people had worked, their names still on gummed labels that hadn't quite washed off the desks. I had known and liked the *Form* guys in the box for years, but watching them do their jobs and even just seeing stacks of *Forms* around them was unbearable.

Fortunately, I soon had alternatives to being surrounded by journalists with jobs and to using the *Form*. After being turned away by the *Form,* Equibase had begun supplying past-performance lines to some Eastern tracks, and New York was among the first to start publishing them in the track program. So I didn't have to use the *Form* and went back to enhancing raw running lines with my own figures and research, the way I had throughout the 1980's.

For a base of operations away from the press box, I joined the Turf and Field Club, a dying vestige of the days when private clubs had flourished within racetracks to insulate the socialites from the grandstand gamblers. The Turf and Field was now open to anyone willing to pay $1,000 a year, and while it barely attracted a dozen members on weekdays, it still had its own spacious dining rooms at Aqueduct and Belmont where I could spread out my handicapping tools and focus on the races in virtual isolation.

The only drawbacks were the room's anachronistic requirement of a jacket and tie, and the $20 daily food-and-beverage minimum, an unwelcome piece of overhead in my new line of business. Now that I was paying my own way, I better understood the griping of the regulars about how poorly racing treated its best customers.

It wasn't that the $6,000 a year in membership and lunch bills was going to make or break anyone's year, but why were we paying *anything* for the privilege of having our hosts extract 20 percent from our total handle? At a casino, a customer who loses $100,000 a year is treated like a sultan, housed in hotel suites, and fed free meals from the gourmet restaurant. A bettor who pushes $2,000 a day through the windows, 250 days a year, is a $500,000-a-year customer who is "losing" $100,000 to the house right off the top of his handle. He doesn't get so much as a free coffee mug, and on top of that he has to pay for a place to sit and a pot of coffee.

I was working even more obsessively on my figures and record-keeping than ever. I now had three spiral-bound books filled with thousands of razor-tipped pen strokes—my Derby book, my daily New York book of results, and now an additional book breaking down the fractional and final times for nearly 100 horses a day. Any civilian accidentally walking into the Turf and Field and seeing me hunched over these notebooks would probably have assumed I was one of those lunatics you see in the subway, carefully recording the secret codes that aliens are beaming to their brains.

Despite all the work I was doing, the new enterprise was not going well. A year and a half away from watching every race every day had made me unfamiliar with the current crop of daily runners. I realized that visual observations had been a more important part of my handicapping than I might have acknowledged. I could play the game pretty well from afar, but to make the correct fine-line decisions in a bet such as the pick six, I needed to know practically every horse on the grounds and remember small details about his recent races.

By June I had lost most of my Maxwell severance money. It had been a strange spring, the first time in 11 years that I had not attended the Derby or watched the Belmont from the press box. I was feeling more and more caught up on New

York racing, but I hadn't made a big score. A paying job was starting to sound like good idea.

On June 16, there was a one-day carryover at Belmont and the card didn't look too promising because the pick-six sequence began with two imposing favorites, and two later races appeared to have stickouts as well. Still, I played my usual array of mains, backups, double backups, triple backups, and extra-super backups, making out 24 tickets for a total investment of $1,980.

About 20 minutes before the pick six began, it was announced that the heavy favorite in the first leg had been scratched. He had been a single on many of my tickets and I had to tear up all 24 slips and start over. The first race was now wide open, and using several horses instead of one meant narrowing down elsewhere. I frantically devised a new strategy for the day and concocted an array of tickets in which two of the three remaining favorites had to win. I was scribbling frantically, and by the time I was done I was up to 32 tickets and $2,782.

The scratched favorite in the first leg had been a dominant speedball, and one of the horses I had added in his absence, Penny's Buck, was now the lone front-runner. He walked to the lead and held on to pay $13.80. The next winner paid $17 and the third leg ended with a photo-finish between the 3-5 favorite and a 6-1 shot I had used only as a backup. The 6-1 shot got the nod and I was alive with three good prices behind me, but in terrible position. I was down to a single ticket, one that combined my backups in the second and third legs with thinned-down mains the rest of the way. I would have to crawl home on my belly with a shallow ticket that was only 1 x 1 x 2.

You rarely get there with such sparse coverage, but this time everyone I needed had a perfect trip and ran to his figures.

After getting my two singles home, I watched my two horses in the finale run 1-2 every step of the way around the track with no one else close.

There was always a two-minute gap between the last leg of the pick six and the posting of the payoff, a tantalizing suspension of time when you're sitting on a winner but can only guess at the price. Multiplying the odds of all the individual winners usually puts you in the ballpark, but the actual payoff, which is simply the pool divided by the number of winning tickets, can deviate greatly. A 6-5 favorite might be half that price in the pick six if a lot of people singled him. A succession of second and third choices can pay less than the odds suggest if they won races in which everyone used the same two or three obvious horses.

I ran through the possibilities with Robin, who had made a rare weekday trip to the races with me. I lowballed just a little, telling her I thought the payoff would be $20,000 when I was secretly hoping for $30,000. So I was a little disappointed when the price was posted as $16,276.40.

Someone a few tables away who knew I had hit it let out a congratulatory whoop that seemed excessive for the payout. I looked back at the tiny television screen at my table and saw I had missed a zero. I was the only winner and the payoff was $162,760.40.

I didn't go to Disneyland. We went out to dinner and had some champagne, but I followed that up with several cups of coffee so I could go home and handicap the next day's card. It had been a good day at the office, and a needed morale boost after a long losing streak, but what most people would consider a life-changing jackpot was just a necessary infusion of cash for my new career. The $162,760.40 would diminish quickly, with the government taking nearly $45,000 off the top, my replacing the $40,000 in losses of the three prior months, and $20,000 in Saratoga expenses looming now that there was no *New York Times* or *Racing Times* to pay my way.

I felt that the best thing about it was not the money, but the vindication for all the hours of scribbling and studying, and the fact that my first year as a "professional" horseplayer would be a winning one, even if I went cold for the rest of the year.

The game was beatable, but it was far from the fantasy of easy riches so many people have. I would spend nearly three years as an almost daily Turf and Field attendee and got to know many of the regulars who were betting seriously. The few long-term winners were extremely smart people who did hours of daily homework, and they still might not have as much to show for it at the end of the year as they would have from cashing a paycheck at a modest job.

I had always imagined there was a substantial network of professional players who earned regular and handsome profits at the track year after year, but I came to believe that there is at best a handful. Most recreational horseplayers share my initial misconception and believe there is an all-knowing circle of such winners. This is why so many players study the tote boards and probable payoffs looking for signs of the "inside dope" and the "smart money" when in fact there is very little of either.

As I got to know the regulars, it became clear that few were truly supporting themselves this way. Even the braggarts who said they beat the game consistently often turned out to be living off an inheritance or a wealthy spouse, or at least a recent insurance settlement. There's an almost infallible rule of thumb equating how a horseplayer says he's doing with how he's actually doing. Those who are losing claim they're breaking even. Those who are breaking even claim to be way ahead of the game. Those who really do win say very little—except that the game is humbling and that betting horses is a very tough way to make a living.

I was doing something I enjoyed and happy to be ahead, but I would have swapped the pick-six ticket in a heartbeat to still be putting out *The Racing Times*—not that there was a chance of ever getting a racing paper back. On the richest day of my life, that $162,760.40 seemed awfully small when I made the depressing calculation of what it would take to get back into that business. I would have to hit 125 pick sixes that big to come up with the $20 million Maxwell had put into *The Racing Times*, and more than 1,500 of them to get to the $250 million that K-III had paid for the *Form*.

THAT SUMMER THE *Form* added the Beyer figures to its past performances and I decided that was my cue to develop some new data of my own. Several figure-makers had only half-jokingly said I had ruined their edge by putting the Beyers into *The Racing Times,* and now, after a few months' absence, they were in the only surviving paper. I thought making my own figures still gave me an advantage over people using the Beyers without having done any work of their own, but having high-quality figures so widely available meant that my 6-5 standouts would soon be everyone else's 3-5 singles.

It was time for me to tackle the thorny issue of pace. For all my fussing and precision with final running times, my approach to early speed in races was no more sophisticated than occasionally noticing that a horse like Penny's Buck had a lot of 1's at the early calls in his past performances. I knew, as any rational horseplayer does after watching his first 1,000 races, that an absence of early speed in a field helped a front-runner get a soft trip on the lead while an abundance of front-runners meant there might be a taxing early duel that would tire them all out.

That was as scientific as I had been, though, and it had always nagged at me that there had to be a better way to quantify pace than to look at misleading running lines. My whole approach to time had been that speed figures revealed truths behind the optical illusions of victories and raw times—so why was I gauging pace based only on whether a horse had "finished first" in the race for the early lead?

Just as I had skipped over the math of speed figures when I had first read Beyer a decade earlier, I had read Tom Brohamer's seminal *Modern Pace Handicapping* without absorbing its arcane arithmetic for quantifying a horse's early speed. Now I went back and studied it like a textbook. While I ultimately disagreed with its suggested methodology, the thoughtful book set off a number of bells in my head and made me rethink the game once again.

I had always emotionally preferred stretch-runners to front-runners, ever since choosing Alydar over Affirmed. Even knowing that many late runs were optical illusions, I had instinctively sided with these underdogs, who had to overcome a disadvantage. Obviously I respected and often wagered on front-runners when that made sense, but like many horseplayers, I would rather be rooting for a late charger to get up than for an exhausted leader to hang on.

Brohamer's book, and its attempt to quantify fractional time as well as overall time, began to push me in the other direction. Which is the worthier winning performance: one by a horse that runs six furlongs in 1:12 after a half-mile in 46 seconds, or one that runs the same 1:12 after a half in 46⅗? I had always chosen the drama of the latter horse's faster finish, but objectively, a horse that runs more taxing early fractions has run the more admirable race.

The idea took hold that if I could quantify that superiority, I could apply it profitably. If I could make a separate speed figure for the first part of a horse's effort, as well as his overall performance, I might have something to work with. I now might view those two horses' identical final-time performances as follows:

	PACE TIME	FINAL TIME	PACE FIG	FINAL FIG
Horse A	46	1:12	55	50
Horse B	46⅗	1:12	46	50

The implications of having a second figure for each horse were revelatory. I began looking at these two horses not as a pair of 50's, but at Horse A as having 105 (55 + 50) "ability points" and Horse B as having only 96. In theory, this meant that Horse A's final performance depended in effect on how he rationed those points during the running of a race. If he ran a 55 early, he would do no better than a final 50.

But what if he was tractable, and a race came up with an absence of other front-runners, so that he could get away with running only a 50 early? Now he might well be able to run a final figure of 55.

It seemed to work the other way as well. A horse that had gotten away with an easy lead through slow fractions to earn pace and final figures of 40 and 50 might be heavily favored next time because none of his opponents had run a final figure faster than 50. Facing more and better speed, though, he might now be pushed into a 50 early and thus a final figure of 40, which would be too slow to win the race.

It was fascinating stuff and gave a third dimension to my handicapping. I was now routinely betting against the horse with the top final-time figure if he had achieved it in conjunction with a weak pace figure, and found myself backing horses I once would have dismissed as quitters.

I also had doubled my figure-making workload. In addition to calibrating the speed of the racing surface based on final times, I now had to make a separate pace variant for each day, and to calculate two figures for each horse's performance. I was becoming more of a hermit by the day, and taking even a couple of days off would leave me with a mountain of work to catch up on. For the first time, "doing the work" was something I almost dreaded rather than enjoyed.

Then I got lucky and met David Ward. A programmer who had designed computer systems for banks and insurance companies in the Boston area, Ward was an enthusiastic recreational horseplayer who saw racing as a game and an industry perfectly cut out for technology it was not using. He thought past performances were ideally suited for the personal computers that were starting to make their way into people's homes.

He had approached tracks and industry organizations about developing products and planning for a future that might include something called the Internet, and was turned away by all of them. He had been a big fan of *The Racing Times,* and in frustration turned to me for help. Perhaps we could collaborate on a computer-based handicapping product.

After a few meetings, it was clear to me that Ward was on to something big in the long run and also could simplify my life by hours a day in the short run. It sounded like a monumental project, but was in fact a snap for him to design a program just like the one we had labored over at *The Racing Times* with the Beyer figures. I now could enter my winning pace and final figure for each race just once, and any time a horse ran back, Ward's program would calculate that horse's figures. He arranged it so they could be automatically inserted into electronic past performances, and my home printer could create a customized *Form* for me with all my figures in it, saving me three hours a day of drudge work. Sharing my figures with him for his own research and horseplaying was all he wanted in return.

It was like having my own personal past-performance newspaper, albeit one with an unpaid national circulation of two. Ward still couldn't interest anyone in developing the application for commercial use and we ended up sharing it with a few other people, including Beyer and Mark Hopkins, and personalizing it further for each handicapper's areas of interest. He added a capability to record trip notes on a race, which would then pop up every time the horse ran instead of the *Form*'s one- or two-word comment. We also began adding statistics on the trainer of each horse and inserting these below the past-performance lines.

Ward's program simplified my life and gave me back hours that I soon needed for some unpaid work I couldn't turn down: a chance to do something about some of the injustices I believed horseplayers suffered.

IN 1988, NEW YORK'S jockeys had staged a brief strike, a labor action that went nowhere because owners and trainers had no trouble recruiting out-of-town substitutes who thought nothing of crossing a picket line for a shot at richer purses and better horses. During the week-long strike, I got to know the jockeys' spokesman, an attorney named Brian Meara, who appreciated a sympathetic ear when others in the press were depicting the riders as ungrateful millionaires.

Four years later, Meara was a legislative aide and lobbyist in Albany when Governor Mario Cuomo announced he was forming a nine-man "blue-ribbon panel" to study racing in New York and make recommendations for its future. Cuomo would appoint three panelists including the chairman, Vincent Tese, and gave three selections to each of the two leaders of the state legislature: Ralph Marino, president of the Republican-controlled state senate, and Saul Weprin, speaker of the Democratic-controlled assembly.

The appointees were mostly businessmen such as Tese, or politicians, including a senator and an assemblyman. Each of the three appointers, however, made one selection of someone who was familiar with racing. Cuomo tapped Robert Sise, an upstate lawyer and horseplayer whose son trained a small stable at Belmont; Marino picked John Tatta, a co-founder of Cablevision who had put the Harvey Pack show on the air and went to the track every weekend. Weprin asked Brian Meara for a suggestion, and Meara proposed an unemployed horseplayer who used to write for *The New York Times*.

Weprin called me in for an interview and we hit it off right away. An elderly liberal Democrat beloved in his working-class Queens district, Weprin said he knew plenty of horseplayers and liked the idea of putting me on the commission "with the money boys and the stuffed shirts." He gave me a quick and brutally frank rundown on the politics of New York racing.

Like everything else in the state, he said, racing was a football in the usual scrum between Democrats and Republicans. The commission would be a political snakepit and would boil down to a fight over the New York Racing Association, the not-for-profit entity packed with Jockey Club types that operated Aqueduct, Belmont, and Saratoga under a state franchise due to expire in a few years. He told me that Cuomo wanted to see NYRA dismantled and replaced by a state agency, while the Republicans were NYRA backers, at least partly because some NYRA board members were longtime and generous political contributors to the Republicans.

The only thing bipartisan was that both parties considered the state OTB system a godsend for rewarding political backers and friends, and that was why OTB had been set up in such a bizarre fashion when it began back in 1971. The state's first choice had been to let the tracks operate OTB, but NYRA, under the leadership of Alfred Vanderbilt, had turned them down flat. Vanderbilt, who was passionate about the sport and worked tirelessly to improve it, was much less enthusiastic about wagering and said that NYRA was in the racing and not the gambling business.

It was a fateful miscalculation, one of the few in Vanderbilt's distinguished career. Instead of controlling its retail outlets, NYRA ended up at war with them in a battle for customers. NYRA got more money for purses and operations from a bet placed at the track than at an OTB, and OTB got nothing from a bet placed at the track. So NYRA spent millions telling people to come to the track while OTB urged them to bet around the corner, instead of having a single entity promoting the game to all. You couldn't even cash a ticket bought at the track at an OTB, or vice versa.

Left to run OTB on its own, the state followed every wrong, greedy, bureaucratic instinct. Rather than having a single statewide operation, it created six separate corporations, one each for New York City, Nassau County, Suffolk County, and the Catskill, Capital, and Western regions. The wastefulness of having six of everything, from computer systems to legal departments, paled next to the bounty of having six times as many jobs to hand out.

Weprin was skeptical about undoing 20 years of systematic corruption, and acknowledged that even good-government proponents like him would have political trouble trying to streamline a system that had been as generous to organized labor as to politicians in creating unnecessary jobs. Still, he said, it was worth a try because the expiration of the NYRA franchise might be an opportunity for change.

The commission was named and introduced at an October press conference, and we had our first meeting a few days later. Chairman Tese told us that Cuomo wanted our report by June of 1993. He then asked how often we thought we should meet over the next nine months. I assumed it was a question of how many days a week.

"Once a month seems about right," said one of the appointees, and I started to laugh at what I thought was a joke, until I noticed everyone else was nodding as if this were a perfectly reasonable and appropriate workload. All that we would do would be to hold some hearings, chat a few times, and then issue a report.

At the first hearing, the leaders of NYRA and each of the OTB's came and read prepared statements about what fine organizations they ran and how well they served the public. The commissioners asked few and perfunctory questions and I wore out everyone's patience by asking each OTB chieftain why the state needed six separate companies to run a statewide betting system. They insisted with straight faces that six operations were necessary to serve the "differing regional needs" of the customers.

Two more sets of hearings, downstate and upstate, drew fewer and fewer of my fellow commissioners and an increasingly odd assortment of people who wanted to testify. There were several civic-minded fans with long lists of complaints about the way the game was conducted, but they were out-numbered by special-interest groups such as harness-racing proponents seeking a bailout for their moribund industry and antigambling moralists who wanted all racing shut down.

After the hearings, Tese broke the group into three committees to focus on key issues and prepare draft reports proposing legislative changes. I suggested a fourth one devoted to betting and was put in charge of it. I no longer had much hope that the commission was going to restructure racing in New York, but perhaps I could at least press for a few parimutuel changes. The two other commissioners assigned to my committee told me to go ahead and suggest whatever I wanted and they would probably go along with it. Tese advised me to keep it simple and limit myself to three specific proposals. I chose withholding taxes, breakage, and takeout.

Getting rid of the state withholding taxes on gambling winnings was surprisingly easy to argue. Once I laid out how horseplayers were having their working capital confiscated by being treated as one-time lottery winners every time they cashed an exotic bet, the economists on the panel immediately grasped how unfair and regressive the tax really was.

Breakage, the ancient practice of rounding down payouts to the nearest 20-cent increment, had been a pet cause of mine since my early days as a show bettor. There was no way to get rid of it entirely. Tracks were not going to start using pennies and slow down the betting lines to pay $4.57 instead of $4.40, and the state was not going to give up the $6 million a year it skimmed from all the rounding. It occurred to me, however, that there was a way to maintain most of the revenue while making breakage fairer.

What had initially outraged me about breakage was that rounding $2.39 on a $2 bet down to $2.20 was stealing 19 cents from what should have been a 39-cent profit—nearly half of the bettor's winnings. It wasn't the 19 cents—it was the 47 percent. What if breakage were applied on a sort of sliding scale instead of rounding down every payout regardless of size? When my pick six had paid $162,760.40, I never would have known or cared if the 40 cents to the right of the decimal point had disappeared. Even $60.40 could have been shaved off the top.

So why not institute smaller breakage increments on small payouts such as show bets and bigger ones on larger payoffs? Why not round $2.37 down to $2.30 instead of $2.20, but round down $487.48 to a flat $487? This too proved an easy sell to my fellow commissioners.

Takeout was the most important of the three areas, addressing the fundamental economic structure of the game. In every type of organized gambling there is a takeout, the percentage of the gross pool that comes off the top, either in the form of a mathematical edge for the house in fixed-odds casino games, or as a direct withdrawal from the pool to cover expenses, as in racing. For every dollar bet at the track, somewhere between 15 and 25 percent (depending on the bet type and each state's legislation) is removed from the pool, and the holders of winning tickets split up what's left over.

This 15 to 25 percent takeout rate is high in the world of gambling. The house edge at a casino is as low as 2 percent at blackjack, around 3 percent at roulette, and 4.54 percent for those betting football games with legal or illegal sports bookmakers. A rate as high as 25 percent is exceeded only by state lotteries, which grab as much as 50 percent.

Racing's high takeout rate is what makes long-term victory so difficult, perhaps close to impossible. Takeout takes its bite race after race, slowly but inevitably transferring the customers' money to the house. If the public begins the day with a total of $1 million in its pockets and bets it all on the first race, the track takes $200,000 and redistributes the remaining $800,000 to the holders of winning tickets. If the public reinvests that money on the second race, it loses another $160,000 and has only $640,000 left—and so on and so on. Eventually, everyone would be flat broke and the house would have the whole $1 million if the track didn't eventually close down for the day, giving the bettors a chance to go home and get fresh money.

Lowering the rate of takeout would mean smaller immediate cuts for the track and the state, but numerous studies had shown that betting would soon increase because the total public would have more money to reinvest. NYRA had been a leader on this issue and twice convinced the legislature to lower takeout during the 1980's to test the theory. Both times betting increased, but both times the bills had been short-term experiments that got lost in the shuffle when it came time for renewal.

NYRA, to its credit, had continued to press for a takeout reduction. Its lone but powerful opponents were the OTB's, where no one was willing to risk a short-term revenue hit that might lead to a reduction of patronage jobs. With practically every OTB appointment subject to change every two years depending on election results, no one wanted to give the other political party an opportunity to make an issue out of declining revenues.

My withholding, breakage, and takeout-reduction recommendations went straight into a draft of the commission report that we all saw for the first time two weeks before it was scheduled to be issued. They were nuggets next to the monumental overarching recommendation that the full commission had barely discussed: As Saul Weprin had predicted, Cuomo's major goal had been to suggest transferring NYRA's authority to a new state-run entity.

The plan was released June 1, 1993, and was dead on arrival. The statewide Republicans were not going to let NYRA disappear, and the local politicians wanted to leave the OTB system just the way it was. The entire exercise had been something of a charade.

That summer, the state legislature began the annual process of reviewing and renewing the racing statutes. Like the takeout-reduction experiments, most New York racing bills to this day have unnecessarily short lives, a cynical custom with the sole purpose of making everyone in the industry come to Albany each year to beg and bargain. The new plan was not even seriously considered, and the OTB's vetoed the takeout-reduction recommendation. At least the state withholding taxes would be repealed and I still had a shot on the breakage issue.

I had remained in touch with Rich Rosenbush at the *Times* throughout the commission's work, and he suggested I write a guest column for the sports section's new Sunday op-ed page about how it had all turned out. I filed a dismayed piece criticizing the intentions and result of the commission's work and expressing the hope that in the absence of changing the racing landscape, the legislature might still address a few crumbs such as breakage for the horseplayers.

The day the piece ran, I was sitting in the Turf and Field making out my pick-six tickets when I was paged for a phone call. When an unfamiliar voice said "Please hold for Governor Cuomo," I wondered which of my wiseacre friends was calling looking for a piece of my ticket. Even after Cuomo's unmistakable voice came on the line, I asked him twice if it was really him.

He wasn't thrilled about the article, but said he'd see what he could do about my pet breakage issue. What he really wanted to tell me, he said, was that NYRA was the real enemy and that he was disappointed I didn't seem to share his desire to dissolve it. NYRA, he said, represented much of what he had fought against for his entire political career—an entrenched, privileged board of bluebloods and millionaires using their wealth and influence to retain their power.

"They're really bad guys," he said several times in the course of keeping me on the phone for 20 minutes and making me miss the deadline for getting in pick-six tickets. Fortunately, I would have been knocked out in the first leg, so the governor's legendary long-windedness ended up saving me $1,500.

My breakage plan was signed into law a month later. No other state in the union has adopted it, but I still smile every time a horse at a New York track pays $9.90 instead of $9.80, and especially when a show bet pays $2.30 instead of $2.20.

CUOMO EXTENDED THE life of the commission for another six months, which allowed us to file two more reports and another proposal for takeout reduction that went straight to the state archives without being given any more serious consideration. As 1994 began, I thought I was through with politics, and even with NYRA as anything but a paying customer and freelance journalist.

Several of my *Racing Times* deputies had eventually found their way into editorships and were kind enough to throw their old boss some work. Irwin Cohen was now working for *Playbill* and had created an editorial wraparound for the NYRA track program that included a new betting column from me every two weeks. Ray Paulick had been named the editor in chief of *The Blood-Horse* and had made me its New York correspondent, writing the same kind of weekly roundup I had done for *The Thoroughbred Record* a decade earlier. The two jobs added up to less than I had made as a reporter in my rookie year, but I enjoyed writing again, was happily ensconced in the Turf and Field, and wasn't broke yet.

While the Cuomo commission had been up and running, I had been wary of friendly approaches from track officials who might be trying to influence me, but after that was all over I continued to get regular visits in the Turf and Field from Allan Dragone, who had succeeded Dinny Phipps and Thomas Bancroft Jr. as NYRA's chairman in 1990. Dragone had been the president of Celanese Corporation and vice chairman of Burlington Industries before retiring to pursue his favorite hobby. He bred and owned horses and also liked to handicap and make small bets to keep score. He loved the game as much as he hated the politics of New York racing that kept him from running NYRA the way he had run Celanese—as a real business rather than some immovable, quasi-governmental bureaucracy.

Dragone was the first business executive I got to know well, and his approach was refreshing. Problems in racing weren't something just to get up on a soapbox and complain about, but specific challenges to be analyzed and acted upon, and as soon as possible. He liked imaginative and unconventional thinking, and I could see that one of his strengths as a chief executive had been shaping other people's vague ideas into something achievable, the way a good editor reins in and helps a talented but rough writer. We began talking several times a week.

One day, out of nowhere, Dragone asked me if I might like to come to work for NYRA. He didn't have a particular job in mind but wanted me "on the team." I told him I was flattered to be asked and that the idea had some appeal, but that for now I was happy writing and gambling and couldn't see myself fitting into a corporate structure.

He asked that I humor him and meet with a friend of his, an executive recruiter he had used to evaluate prospective employees. He said he thought that at worst it would be an entertaining meeting, and that I had nothing to prove or lose since I didn't want a job anyway.

I met with the woman a few weeks later. Since I wasn't trying to provide the "right" answers, I basically unloaded on NYRA and what I saw as the failings of its executives in serving the betting public. She asked me all sorts of hypothetical questions about collaboration and teamwork and how I had set things up at *The Racing Times,* and our two hours together went by quickly.

About a week later, Dragone came to me and said he was glad I hadn't wanted a job. While his friend had enjoyed our session, she strongly recommended against trying to turn me into a corporate executive. She had concluded I was an entrepreneur rather than a team player, lacked the patience for corporate procedures, and would be a risky hire because I was anti-authoritarian and my loyalties would always be suspect.

I recalled that she had asked me, "What would you do if your superior told you to support a position you personally disagreed with?" I had insisted this was an unanswerable trick question because I was confident I could talk him out of the incorrect decision. I think this was the wrong answer.

"We think you'd make a great chairman but not such a great employee," was how Dragone summed it up, "and you can't have my job. But let's keep talking."

I took her evaluation as a compliment. I realized how lucky I was never to have been on the short end of a traditional employee-boss relationship or been put into positions like the hypotheticals she had posed. At *The New York Times,* I had worked from the field and my bosses had been sympathetic editors who left me alone and let me tell them what I should be doing. At *The Racing Times,* my only charge had been to develop the best possible newspaper. George White had shielded me from the business issues of the startup, and while Maxwell was a tyrant of a boss, he usually could be ignored and allowed to sleep off his worst ideas. Even on the Cuomo commission, I had been sent off on my own to devise proposals that went into not only the report, but also the statutes, virtually unchanged.

At the same time, I wasn't crazy about being told I was incapable of doing something. I began to think it might be worth trying, if only to prove the recruiter wrong. Besides, the idea of finding out how a racetrack really worked from the inside had me more than a little curious, and perhaps I could more effectively agitate for change from within the system. I began to regret not having told the recruiter what she wanted to hear, if only to have the opportunity to decide whether this was worth a try.

The 1994 Saratoga meeting was a business and public-relations disaster. NYRA had dodged a bullet with the Cuomo commission, but the question of whether NYRA was the best outfit to be operating racing in the state was now on the public's mind, and NYRA executives didn't help things by being relentlessly defensive and combative with the once-supportive beat reporters, who over the years had turned against management.

On closing day at Saratoga, Dragone shook up the executive team and dismissed the chief operating officer, then called me into his office. He said more changes were on the way and when it was all over he wanted me on the team, regardless of what the recruiter had said. He mentioned a generous starting salary and a vice presidency of something to be determined later. Having learned from the Maxwell experience never to take anyone's first offer, I told him that the salary sounded a little low but I was sure we could work something out.

We shook hands and then nothing happened for six weeks. I continued playing the races and writing my pieces and waiting for Dragone to tell me when to report for work. There was widespread speculation that Gerry McKeon, NYRA's president for the last 12 years, was also on his way out, but in early October Dragone invited me to join him and McKeon for brunch. He said McKeon had resisted the idea of hiring me but had finally come around. We shook hands on a still unspecified vice-president's job, and McKeon said he'd call me in a few days. Dragone said with a mischievous twinkle in his eye that "things are about to get interesting."

McKeon didn't call that week, and the following Monday NYRA announced a press conference for Thursday. I called Dragone to tell him that I hadn't heard from McKeon and we really needed to sort out a deal if they were announcing my hiring Thursday. He told me that the press conference was about something else and to sit tight.

That night, the phone rang just after nine o'clock at home. "Hey Steve, it's Kenny Noe."

I hadn't talked to Kenny since I had worked at *The New York Times*. He had been a racing secretary at several tracks, including NYRA's, before my time, and was semi-retired now after a long career as a racing official and track operator. The stories I had heard were that he was a hard-working, old-school racing official who was proud to be considered a dinosaur in the new world of simulcasting and exotic betting. He had found a perfect spot for himself running Calder

Race Course, the least glamorous but most profitable of the Miami area's three racetracks. Calder was never part of the annual battle over midwinter racing dates between Hialeah and Gulfstream, and operated quietly from May to December. I had called him once for comment on the annual dates battle sometime during the 1980's, and he'd had some fun with me.

"You must have a wrong number," he had said when I identified myself. "We're just a bunch of farmers trying to run a little bitty racetrack down here in peanut country and I can't imagine why *The New York Almighty Times* would be calling me up. This must be something important."

Now, almost 10 years later, he was the one with something important to tell me.

"Listen," he began, "they're going to make an announcement tomorrow and then there's a press conference Thursday at noon and then I'm going to the Breeders' Cup and I've got some commitments after that but then we should sit down and talk."

I was furiously scribbling down what he was saying, taking notes like a reporter, but with no idea where this was all going.

"Well yeah, they're going to make the announcement that I'm coming in as president and general manager of N-Y-R-A," he said, spelling out the acronym. "I guess they call it 'Nye-ruh' up there but I prefer N-Y-R-A. I don't know, I've been dealing with the press for 30 years and I know you're press. I don't know why they don't like me. I guess it's because I tell the truth. Someone tried to congratulate me on this thing but I don't know, it looks like they've got a lot of problems up there. You were with *The New York Times*, right, and then you started that other thing?"

"*The Racing Times*."

"Right, you had some good articles but I couldn't make heads or tails out of the rest of it. So I understand you're interested in coming on board at N-Y-R-A."

My head was spinning.

"I'm a little confused here," I finally said. "I don't know how much Allan Dragone's told you about the conversations we've already had and—"

"No, he hasn't told me much, he just told me to give you a call. So send me a resume, okay buddy? You take care."

I was completely confused now. I went to the Thursday press conference and stood in the back of the room as Kenny was introduced to a new generation of New York reporters. I caught Dragone's eye and he shrugged and turned his palms up, as if to say I was on my own. I reintroduced myself to Kenny after the press conference and he pulled me aside.

"I've been here for two days and let me tell you, this is the most screwed-up organization I've ever seen in my life," he said. "I don't know if it's too far gone to fix it. You come see me when I'm back in town in a couple of weeks and we'll talk."

Five days later, an upset came in a race away from the track that cast doubt on whether NYRA had made the right choices in changing its management team. Cuomo was up for reelection and had been considered a shoo-in. McKeon had, very early and very publicly, backed the governor's longshot opponent, an obscure Peekskill politician named George Pataki. McKeon had been roundly criticized for taking an apparently hopeless public position that would only further antagonize a reelected Cuomo against NYRA.

Cuomo, however, had somehow managed to wear out his popularity, and three days after the Breeders' Cup, Pataki scored a surprising victory over the man who probably could have been president of the United States two years earlier had he opposed Bill Clinton for the nomination. McKeon had been unexpectedly vindicated but had been replaced a week earlier.

I also wondered whether I fit into the new scheme, not only because of Kenny's arrival but also because of Cuomo's defeat. Back in August and September, when everyone had expected a Cuomo reelection, perhaps I had been seen as a cushion against his likely wrath at NYRA for having opposed him in public. The truth was that Cuomo was annoyed at me about the *Times* piece, but people at NYRA seemed to think I had an inside track with him and the Democratic Party.

When I met with Kenny a week after the election, I told him I understood there had been regime changes both at NYRA and in Albany since I had shaken hands on a job with the former president and current chairman. I didn't want to work there if they didn't want me and I'd be happy to go back to writing and betting. His response surprised me.

"A handshake's all that counts, so if you got one you're working here if you still want," he said. "Now let's figure out what you're going to do. I don't know much about you except that Dinny and Allan seem to like you, and you're a race-tracker, so you and I should get along okay. Hell, you couldn't be any worse than most of the people they've got working here. Welcome aboard, pardnuh. Now we just gotta get you some handcuffs."

Handcuffs?

"To keep you away from the betting windows," he said with a laugh. "Do what you want on your own time or when you go out of town, but employees can't be betting our races while they're working here."

This had never come up in my previous conversations with Dragone and McKeon, and it hadn't occurred to me whether I was willing to give up the hobby that had become a passion and, most recently, my primary means of support. I quickly decided that I was. Serious handicapping was something I could always come back to, and after nearly three years without a job it would be a relief not to have my financial security hinging on each day's pick six. A vacation from the gambling life didn't seem like such a bad idea, but what an odd place to take it—at the same tracks where I had been betting almost every day for nearly 15 years.

THE ODD COUPLE

K ENNY AND I SETTLED on a title of "Director of Communications and Development," an umbrella for the various departments that would report to me: marketing, simulcasting and television, media relations, the track program, and customer service. I wouldn't be a vice president because "this place has too many goddamn vice presidents and by law I've only got to have one." In his first month, Kenny fired or demoted NYRA's five other VP's, including one the day before he announced my hiring: Allen Gutterman, the extremely popular head of the marketing department.

Kenny and I went up to the press box the next day to announce that I was coming to work for NYRA. He took the heat for firing the well-liked Gutterman and told the press that I had nothing to do with it and that he had decided to eliminate the position.

"I never quite understood what that job meant anyway," he said. "I always thought 'marketing' was what my wife did down at the store."

I cringed, realizing that this was what Dragone and Phipps had meant in recent days when they had told me that Kenny was going to be a tough sell to the New York press. Before day's end, I found myself already being a spin doctor, telling an offended woman reporter that from what I knew of Kenny, his remark had been an attempt at gentle humor and did not reflect his professional attitude toward women in racing.

The next day's *Daily Racing Form* carried a bizarrely huge headline: "Crist Takes Over." I couldn't figure out if they were trying to embarrass me, were feeling guilty about *The Racing Times,* or if it had really been that slow a news day. I hadn't "taken over" anything; Kenny had, and I was working for him. When I told Kenny I felt awkward about the headline, he told me not to worry about it.

"That paper's so bad, all I look at is Peb's cartoons," he said.

The Associated Press sent a brief story about my hiring to papers all over the country, which ran it under variations of the headline "Racetrack Hires Gambler," as if Chase Manhattan had named a bank robber to its board of directors. Andy Beyer wrote a *Washington Post* column about the coverage, pointing out that no one would find it odd or amusing if the American Medical Association hired a doctor as an executive and bemoaning the fact that there weren't more bettors, even temporarily retired ones, in track management.

The racing writers and fans seemed to like the idea for exactly that reason, though my former press-box colleagues said it would never last and told me there was an over-under pool going on whether I would survive a year. One columnist called us the Odd Couple, and superficially we were. Kenny was an old-fashioned racing official with a deep distrust and dislike of most of my defining characteristics: New York City, an Ivy League education, newspapers, and gambling. He said he rarely read the papers and was proud not to have read an entire book in 30 years or seen a movie since *Patton* came out.

Yet we hit it off personally right away, perhaps because we shared one thing that transcended our backgrounds: We both were shamelessly sentimental devotees of racing in general and New York racing in particular. We came at it from different directions and different constituencies we were passionate about—Kenny wanted the owners and trainers to have bigger purses, while I wanted the customers to have a better game to play. Perhaps those goals had more in common than in conflict. Or so I told myself.

I knew how to staff and edit a newspaper, but had no idea how to build or lead a corporate division. Dragone wanted me to attend a three-month course at Harvard Business School for new executives, but Kenny snorted and rejected the idea as an expensive waste of time.

"We've got jobs to do here and you don't need to go learn how to pee sitting down," he said. "It's all common sense and hard work and they don't teach that in school."

Most of the NYRA employees were chilly about my arrival. Gerry McKeon had been a popular leader and was being sincere when he said at his retirement dinner that his proudest achievement had been employing all the people in the room over the years and watching them pay their mortgages. NYRA had been a genial and fairly undemanding place to work, with virtually no turnover below the senior-management level.

Now there was this madman from Florida firing people every day, and I was an unlikely part of the new regime.

I was assigned Gutterman's office but spent an awkward first week working at his vacationing secretary's desk as he cleaned out nearly a decade of accumulated possessions and files. His loyalists blamed me for his departure and were barely civil. Within a month, four of them had left for other jobs.

Even after the initial shake-ups, I still had strong department heads, people I had known for years, in three of the five areas that would be reporting directly to me: Marshall Cassidy (of "New York's Easy Goer" fame) in track programs, Cathy Marino in customer service, and Glen Mathes in media relations. I filled the marketing job with Rick Marks, a racing enthusiast and former *New York Times* advertising salesman, and completed the team by reassigning Bill Nader, who had been a marketing assistant, to head up simulcasting and television, the area that had quickly impressed me as having the ripest opportunity for improvements for both NYRA and its customers.

The racing industry had been quietly undergoing a fundamental transformation over the previous three years, ever since a short-lived series of major races for older horses called the American Championship Racing Series had been run in 1991. In the past, the Triple Crown and the Breeders' Cup had been about the only events beamed into tracks around the country and opened to national betting pools. The ACRS had extended that to another 10 races a year and awakened tracks to two key things: Customers enjoyed betting on more out-of-town events, and there was some money to be made by selling the signal of your races to the other tracks.

It was a new and unexpected source of revenue and no one knew what to charge for the signal. In a decision that would come to change the economics of the industry ever since, the tracks sought only a small piece for themselves. They might have demanded half the takeout, or about 9 to 10 percent of the handle, but instead set their prices closer to 3 percent. Perhaps because it seemed like free money, since the only cost was uploading your signal to a satellite, they seemed to think they were entitled to only a small cut, while the receiving track kept almost all the takeout for itself.

It was a boon for smaller tracks with cheap and unappealing live racing of their own. Suddenly they could offer their customers better racing from tracks all over the country, and the only costs were a 3 percent fee to the host track and the price of some additional television monitors. Tracks everywhere became Las Vegas race books, offering action on as many as 20 tracks a day, and venues previously struggling for survival as live-racing operations were showing record profits as legal bookmakers.

Few of them, however, offered NYRA racing. McKeon had taken a stand against the low fees host tracks were receiving and was selling the daily NYRA signal for 6 percent rather than the standard 3 percent. The only regular takers were nearby Eastern markets where the fans would have mutinied without it. McKeon's position was principled and perhaps foresighted, but it was costing NYRA a fortune and diminishing its prominence on the national racing scene.

Bill Nader had come to NYRA from Rockingham Park, a small track in New Hampshire that had benefited greatly from both importing other tracks' signals and selling its own. He knew all the buyers and sellers around the country and that they wanted the NYRA signal if the price could be lowered. I knew how frustrated players in other states were that they couldn't bet on NYRA.

I began studying handle figures and in doing so found an outlet for the arithmetical energies that had gone fallow in the absence of making daily pace and speed figures. I was poring over numbers in the *Form* again—not the ones in the past performances, but each track's daily business figures. I started devoting the hours I previously had spent handicapping to building spreadsheets on where and how horseplayers were betting their money every day—by track, race, type of bet, and on import and export simulcasts.

For an industry that was handling more than $10 billion a year, racing seemed incredibly disorganized and casual about where the money was going. Other than the spare change of admission fees and concession commissions, betting dollars were the sole economic fuel for the tracks, but there was no clearinghouse for essential betting data and little analysis of how customers were investing their money.

It appeared that NYRA could quickly make at least an additional $10 million a year by joining the world of simulcasting. This was 20 times as much as the company would make through Kenny's head-chopping and cost-reduction initiatives, and would make NYRA profitable again. That sort of turnaround would be acclaimed at any conventional company, but as I was quickly learning, there was nothing conventional about how NYRA operated.

NYRA had been established in 1955 as a not-for-profit corporation, privately managed but required to reinvest its earnings or turn them over to the state. There were no real owners demanding profits, and little incentive for the company to do more than break even and perpetuate its existence by keeping the government happy with a stream of income.

The upside to this arrangement was that decisions regarding New York racing did not have to be made for the penny-pinching reasons that drive the for-profit business world. Its managers had literally been able to afford principled decisions about what they thought was best for the sport, or at least how they personally preferred to see racing presented.

The downside was that the utter lack of financial incentive had created a company that was soft and out of touch. NYRA had not had to cheapen itself, but in the absence of pressure to perform better had also unwittingly punished its own customers by ignoring positive changes to the game that just so happened to have been inspired by economic factors elsewhere. Fans wanted simulcasting and more exotic wagers, but NYRA had ignored them, even though these were moneymakers.

Kenny was no fan of simulcasting or exotic betting. He preferred an earlier era in the sport when live racing was all that mattered and when fans filled the stands to watch horses and bet nothing more exotic than a daily double, instead of huddling under television monitors to watch simulcasts and play superfectas. He knew, however, that NYRA had to change in order to continue to exist. He had been brought in by the trustees to shake things up and restore profitability so that the state would not have grounds to dissolve NYRA.

He said he wanted to hold off on bringing in simulcasts for as long as possible, but he gave us the green light to sell the NYRA signal at the prevailing rates. Within a year, practically every track and OTB in the country was offering NYRA racing, and the company had stopped bleeding.

Nader and I realized early on that if the NYRA signal was going to be making its debut all over the country, we would have to build a show around the raw feed of the races. We saw an opportunity to improve on the traditional weakness of simulcast signals, where a genial host would be little more than a traffic director, and instead to use the medium to focus on handicapping and betting.

So we put together a five-hour daily show using both familiar and new talent: Harvey Pack, the broadcast icon of New York racing; Paul Cornman, who had been part of the old Beyer pick-six team and our New York trip-note writer at *The Racing Times*; Mike Watchmaker, whom I had hired as the morning-line maker and handicapper for the track program; Andy Serling, a former options trader who was an obsessive and highly opinionated horseplayer; Jan Rushton, an exercise rider for Shug McGaughey with strong backstretch connections and an eye for the appearance of horses; and John Veitch, who was now training just a few horses after his glory years with Alydar and Calumet Farm.

The finished product ended up having an even wider audience than simulcast sites around the country.

One of the Cuomo commission's recommendations had been to begin experimenting with in-home telecasts of daily racing, and the state legislature had approved the idea. Little had happened, though, because no one could figure out the economics or logistics. Satellite television was in its infancy, and channel space was precious and expensive on cable. The operators of cable systems such as Cablevision and Time Warner wanted a healthy piece of the betting handle in exchange for air time, and had nearly convinced the previous NYRA administration to pay up. The new team took a look at these deals and decided they didn't make any sense.

Kenny was just as happy. He felt that if people could watch the races at home, they were less likely to go to the track, and he thought that better racing and cleaner facilities could reverse a 30-year decline in live attendance. I was convinced, though, that in-home television might be racing's only long-term hope. Racing had missed the boat on television in its early days, and its daily absence from broadcast television had been a big factor in the sport's decline. A constant presence on cable would not only raise racing's visibility but also could attract betting by telephone from people at home or in the office who couldn't make it to the track or an OTB.

The breakthrough idea came from flipping channels at home. On Cablevision of Long Island, the Playboy Channel of soft-core erotica was an additional premium service that broadcast on Channel 67, but there was nothing on that channel before 8:00 P.M. It wouldn't cost Cablevision a nickel to show the races there during the day. If it proved popular enough and really did increase betting, maybe there would be a deal for a piece of the additional handle down the road, but for now why not provide the air space?

For once the OTB's proved an ally and their political clout was a help. It also didn't hurt that John Tatta, Cablevision's co-founder, had been on the Cuomo commission and was a huge racing fan with a few horses and a taste for betting. Cablevision began carrying our daily television show, and many of the state's other cable systems soon joined them. It turned out that every cable system had either a situation like the Playboy Channel, or an empty public-access channel.

New York racing was now freely available in just about every living room in New York State. It was a huge step forward for racing fans but, as usual, they were about to get knocked back a step on another front.

KENNY AND I had started making almost weekly trips to Albany, sometimes joined by Dragone, in an effort to rehabilitate NYRA's image. Kenny was a whirlwind, up at 4:30 every morning, visiting trainers at the track before heading to the airport, talking all the way as we crammed into propeller planes for the 45-minute flight to the state capital. We would spend all day calling on legislators with NYRA's low-key and well-liked lobbyist, Billy Crowell. By late afternoon, Crowell and I would be exhausted from tromping around for hours, but Kenny, nearly 30 years older than either of us, would be suggesting that we visit just a few more people and see if we couldn't take a later flight home.

The New York politicians had never seen anything like him. He'd come bursting into offices, backslapping the men and calling them "buddy" and kissing the women and calling them "hon," and telling the story dozens of times a day that he was here to make friends and to do whatever he could to help New York racing. The politicians thought he was a big, friendly cartoon character and loved him. Those who took him for a rube were making a mistake. Kenny had worked the Florida statehouse for more than a decade and knew exactly what he was doing when he would portray himself as a well-meaning bumpkin.

"It suits me just fine if they think I'm dumb," he once said. "The best way to make a deal is to let the other fella think he's taking advantage of you."

Kenny had been surprisingly flexible about allowing me to pursue simulcasting and in-home betting, issues on which I had expected to get little support. On one trip we were scheduled to meet with state budget officials, and I was hopeful we could make some progress on another of my missions, takeout reduction.

The meeting began badly. The budget chief said that NYRA's contributions to the state had been declining steadily and that while simulcasting and in-home betting were interesting long-term projects, the state wanted more money now. He thought there was an easy solution: New York's 17 percent takeout on straight and two-horse bets was a little low compared to other states. Why not just bump it up to 20 percent?

I saw Dragone's eyes roll back in frustration, and I opened my mouth to begin my stump speech about how takeout was too high already and a reduction was the only path to long-term growth. Kenny jumped in a second before I could begin.

"I couldn't agree with you more," he told the budget chief. "We'd be willing to do that if some of the money came back to us for purses and the facilities."

There was no arguing the point with him or with the state. The bottom line was that if NYRA wanted more purse money and a franchise renewal, the state wanted more money out of the betting pools. Kenny told me to save my breath about how the press and public would react. A few years down the road we could go back and argue for a reduction, but we had to go along with this now or there wouldn't be a NYRA in a few years. The only question was whether the takeout was going up to 19 or 20 percent.

At least I was able to sell them on a scheme that made it look like a restructuring rather than a plain increase. Instead of raising everything from 17 percent to 19 or 20 percent, what if we went from 17 to 20 on two-horse bets such as exactas and daily doubles, but went down from 17 to 15 percent on win, place, and show? Since twice as much was bet on the two-horse wagers, the net effect would be the 2 percent increase they were seeking, but at least this way New York could say it had the lowest win-place-show takeout in the country and we'd be giving takeout-sensitive customers an option.

The idea flew and that summer the legislature signed it into law along with a short-term franchise extension, a renewal of in-home betting, and a very limited menu of incoming simulcasts. The NYRA board was delighted with our positive new relationship with Albany, and the racing press paid more attention to the new low 15 percent takeout on straight wagers than to the onerous 20 percent rate on the more popular bets.

Governor Pataki made a brief appearance at the monthly NYRA board meeting in August at Saratoga, something Cuomo had never done, and praised the organization for its helpful attitude and its support of his administration. It was a lovefest, and after Pataki left, the trustees were happily chattering that this proved that government could be a wonderful partner if you just played ball.

I thought all that it had proved was that the government was for sale and that the customers would always end up footing the bill. I had lost most of my illusions about politics and good government during the Cuomo-commission years, and now I had become convinced that government had little business in racing at all. Why couldn't racing be allowed to operate like any other industry, set its own takeout rates, and make its own business decisions without having to beg and bargain for everything? I now fully understood Dragone's exasperation with the whole process and why he was making the trips to Albany less and less frequently.

As discouraged as I was by Albany politics, I had to pretend that everything was going as well as it could be. Part of my job, the worst part, was being the company's spokesman. The trustees had asked me a few times to keep Kenny away from the press as much as possible because he was always eligible to say something, however well-meaning, that would offend some watchdog of political correctness. Usually that was just fine with Kenny, who didn't have the time or patience for long press conferences and interviews, but when a reporter would phone him directly he felt obliged to take the call and would fire from the hip. The trustees feared that one offhand remark could doom a year's worth of legislative progress.

As the designated apologist for all NYRA activities, I often found the recruiter's question about defending the indefensible ringing in my ears. No one ever asked me to lie, but I sometimes found myself having to justify things the company had done that I thought were bad ideas.

The regular racing writers were no problem. We could talk shorthand and I knew which ones I could trust to tell things off the record for their background without getting burned in print. The only problems came from the generalists or city-desk reporters who would be assigned to cover one racing story a year, often at Saratoga, where any news at the track was a front-page headline in the upstate papers. In August of 1995, they were all over a tiny matter that became a huge story, one on which I was clearly defending the wrong side.

A local artist named Jenness Cortez had for years been painting horse and racetrack scenes. One of her recurring themes was to paint highly realistic panoramas of fantasy races, such as a post parade at Saratoga featuring 19 famous horses from different eras. The race was not real but all the details of the track and the crowd were. These pictures were so popular that she set up a side business reproducing them on T-shirts and greeting cards.

I saw it as free marketing for the track, but NYRA's legal department did not share my enthusiasm. In a masterpiece of bad timing, it hit Cortez with a cease-and-desist order on the eve of the Saratoga meeting, saying she was profiting from illegal and unauthorized use of registered trademarks such as the Saratoga and NYRA logos.

Cortez broadcast the legal letter to every media outlet in

New York and posted fliers around town castigating NYRA for trampling on free speech and bullying a defenseless local artist. So I spent opening day at Saratoga doing one television interview after another in which I was cast as the mouthpiece of the evil corporation. I tried to explain that this was a minor and technical copyright issue, that NYRA had no interest in curtailing anyone's free speech and that we'd like to reach a friendly agreement whereby Cortez might make a small donation to an equine charity in exchange for free use of NYRA property.

That's exactly what we ended up doing, along with giving her space at the track to sell her paintings and merchandise. The image that lingered, though, probably more in my own mind than anyone else's, was of my standing in the blazing sun for those television interviews, sweating and stuffed into a business suit, defending the persecution of a creative artist who liked horse racing.

AFTER BETTING ON New York racing almost every day for 15 years, I had expected to experience withdrawal symptoms by going cold turkey and doing so while spending all day at the track. I was surprised to find that it didn't bother me at all. Playing the races simply wasn't an option, so I didn't feel deprived. I did, however, stumble into a couple of situations where, consistent with my new job, I played the role of the "house" instead of the customer.

The first came one day when I was about to go to Las Vegas for a convention and Kenny called me into his office and gave me $100. He wanted to bet $20 on each of five horses in the Kentucky Derby future book, a bet then offered only by the Vegas casinos. Kenny had picked out horses that he liked or were trained by friends, and he wanted to have something to root for in the Derby season ahead.

I figured that if Kenny could bet on the Derby futures, so could I. So I booked his bet—kept the $100 and rooted against all five of his horses so I wouldn't have to pay off out of my own pocket. When none of them won the Derby, I was up $100 for the year betting on horses.

Another time, a prominent horse owner came to my office and asked if I could get a $4,000 bet down for him on the Super Bowl. I had never bet on sports and didn't have a book-maker, but I had friends who did and thought I would do the owner a favor. The next day a messenger delivered an enve-lope with $4,400 in cash. I threw the envelope in my briefcase and promptly forgot about it—until about five minutes before kickoff. I didn't have a way to reach the owner to tell him I had neglected to place his bet, and that would have been a pretty weaselly thing to do anyway.

I hadn't even planned to watch the game, but now I had no choice but to book the bet and have a strong rooting interest. All I remember about that Super Bowl is that I fell way behind early and didn't rally. I paid off the owner and never told him that his $4,000 profit had come straight out of my bank account.

The end of the legislative season gave me the chance to turn my attention back to the cozier issues of past performances and handicapping—not my own, but what we were providing to our customers as an alternative to the *Daily Racing Form*.

When the *Form* turned down a joint venture with Equibase after *The Racing Times* folded in 1992, Equibase had begun supplying its data to track programs. Only California had declined to use it, leaving the *Form* in strong position there, but in other markets these new past-performance programs were outselling the *Form*. At NYRA in 1995, 50 percent of the customers bought a program and only 17 percent bought the newspaper. The *Form's* stubbornness had created a competitor that couldn't be bought out or shut down and made an enemy of the industry.

The track programs, though, were far from an adequate tool. Most tracks were simply running the raw Equibase data feed and printing it as cheaply as possible without trying to make it a coherent product or a real publication. NYRA's program was one of the best, but had plenty of room for improvement, and I got a fresh taste of being back in the business of putting together a racing publication.

Every track's practice had been to run only as many past-performance lines as would fit on two facing pages. We went to a minimum of 10 lines per horse, just like the *Form*, and sometimes even ran more. Why not run 12 or 14 lines for a six-horse field instead of filling only a page and a half and dropping in an ad for the track's gift shop? We also added a Watchmaker analysis of the card, selections from other handicappers, a wagering grid summarizing what bets were available on each race, and even a racing-news roundup at the front of the book.

Dragone had added me to the Equibase board of directors and I began attending its monthly meetings. The level of hostility toward the *Form* was surprising even to me, and it was clear that if Equibase couldn't bring the *Form* back to the bargaining table, it would bring it to its knees. Sales were dropping 10 percent a year and the company was responding by raising its price while reducing its content and products in cost-cutting moves.

In 1995 the *Form* announced it would no longer publish *The American Racing Manual,* the widely beloved annual almanac that every racing writer and track executive kept on his desk. That gesture alone, which saved the company less than $20,000 a year—barely a rounding error in the overall scheme of things—alienated many of its remaining loyalists and probably cost it 100 times as much in goodwill.

Equibase was in position to deal the *Form* a fatal blow but it didn't, for the same reason that the industry in general had historically moved so slowly. Getting the leaders of so many individual tracks to agree on anything was like herding cats, and Thoroughbred racing lacked a ruling body or league office to make anyone fall into line.

The Equibase board, made up of eight track executives and four Jockey Club officials, was a perfect illustration. Clearly what Equibase needed was an improved and uniform track-program format that was consistent from track to track and could become an industry standard. The $4 *Form* offered only a few things that a $1.50 program didn't—Beyer Speed Figures and a little more handicapping and news. It wouldn't have taken much to close the gap, and then the battle would have been won quickly on price.

The eight track executives, though, could not agree on what a program should look like. Worse, many of them thought that rather than trying to replicate the *Form,* Equibase should create an entirely new product, something supposedly simpler and less "confusing" and "intimidating" than traditional past performances.

The more I got to know these executives, the clearer it became that some of them could barely read the past performances and had no idea that this information was what fueled the betting that was responsible for all their revenue. They seemed to think that their customers were civilians who made impulsive decisions to spend a day in the park looking at horses, and that the future of the game depended on attracting casual customers who might bet $2 a race on names and colors.

Declining business and competition from other forms of gambling had at least awakened track executives to the idea that they might have to do something different. More and more tracks were finally engaging in such fundamentals as market research and increasing their advertising budgets, but to my mind they were going about it the wrong way. They were ignoring the only growth segment in the business—serious players who were betting more than ever through simulcasts. Instead, one track after another brought in marketing directors and consultants from outside the game who took one look at past performances and found them too challenging.

Equibase forged ahead with its new "user-friendly" product called *Bettor Times*, replacing full past performances with bar graphs and pie charts that would supposedly appeal to a younger audience with shorter attention spans and a fondness for *USA Today*-style data snapshots. The product went on sale the following year, never found an audience, and was scrapped.

By then I had been removed from the Equibase board, replaced by Kenny himself. I was wearing out my welcome inside the industry, not only at Equibase but at NYRA as well.

THE FIRST YEAR at NYRA had been packed with change and some legitimate accomplishments, and Kenny and I had gotten along better than anyone had expected or predicted. Our differences had been complimentary when there were so many issues to address, and we had each focused on the areas that played to our strengths and backgrounds.

The recruiter's concerns and my own worries about not

having the temperament for being a corporate executive now seemed silly because Kenny had no interest in, or patience for, traditional business behavior. He set the tone at his first staff meeting, where all the department heads gathered for what they assumed would be an hour or two. One poor soul who arrived literally two minutes late missed the whole thing. Kenny hated meetings. If you had a problem, he said, figure it out or come to him. Meeting over.

From the day he arrived, he said he was in New York for only as long as it took to straighten things out and get a franchise renewal, and then he was headed home to Florida for good to golf in the mornings and spend an occasional day at the races. After that, it would be up to the rest of us to keep New York racing going.

After his first year, Kenny relented on his hatred for vice-presidential titles and promoted me and Terry Meyocks, who had run the racing operations for Kenny at Calder and had come to New York to do the same a few years earlier. The simultaneous promotions to the same title made it appear that Terry and I were now rivals to succeed Kenny, but I never saw it that way. Clearly Kenny wanted Terry, a younger and less extreme version of himself, to head the operation when he left. That was fine with me if my department heads and I could be left alone to run our areas.

After the first year of almost constant projects and crises, though, Kenny began turning his own attention to matters where I previously had a free hand. Dragone could no longer intercede as a voice of moderation. Kenny had demanded the chairman's job and the board had acceded, giving him unprecedented power and, it seemed, a desire to leave his mark on every aspect of the operation before turning it over to Terry.

The daily television show being beamed around the country and into New York homes was a bettor's delight, filled with passionate arguments among handicappers and the occasional skepticism and criticism that horseplayers always bring to the game. To my mind, this frankness gave our product and organization some credibility, but Kenny and Terry saw it as insulting to the horsemen. Every time Harvey Pack would say that a field was weak or that a losing favorite had been awful, my phone would ring and an angry Kenny would demand an end to such disrespect from his employees. Paul Cornman already had quit after a blowup with Kenny, and Pack, Serling, and Veitch were all gone within six months.

The track program became another contentious area. Kenny decided one day that he never wanted to see more than 10 past-performance lines for each horse. End of discussion. He also noticed, a year and a half into Watchmaker's being the line maker, that Mike made selections as well as setting the morning line. Like any handicapper, Mike didn't always like the horse that he knew the public would bet, so he might make a horse the 2-1 favorite but pick someone else in the race.

Kenny called us both in and said he wanted the practice to stop. Mike's "selections" would henceforth be whatever horse he designated as the morning-line favorite, followed by the second choice on the line, followed by the third choice. End of discussion.

Kenny also wanted to try his own hand at advertising and promotion and told me, somewhat ominously, that "you're going to start seeing some things that may surprise you." The first came in August of 1996, a month when the "Macarena" song and dance were a novelty craze. In the middle of a card at Saratoga, the song began booming from every loudspeaker in the plant and the picture on the television monitors cut from the odds board to the winner's circle, where several embarrassed-looking women from the racing office had apparently been pressed into doing the dance.

Kenny dismissed our advertising agency and hired some people from around the track to write and produce a commercial geared at attracting women to the races. The first time I or anyone in the marketing department saw it was when it was broadcast. It opened with a woman unloading a dishwasher and urging the housewives of America to try spending a day at the track.

I probably should have resigned, but I was determined to hang in until they asked me to leave. It didn't take long. Terry was named president of NYRA in December and I was not invited to the January board meeting. Kenny and Terry came back from it and told me they had met with the board's marketing committee, which thought it would be best if I resigned. Within an hour Kenny and I were in the press box, announcing that I had decided to leave NYRA because I felt I had accomplished about all that I could, which was pretty close to the truth.

I knew the story about the marketing committee asking for my resignation was hogwash. Two of its three members were Calvin Klein CEO Barry Schwartz, a longtime supporter of mine and an enthusiastic bettor, and Charlie Hayward, a book publisher with whom I was becoming good friends. Barry phoned me while I was cleaning out my desk to say he had gotten a call from a reporter inquiring about my departure. He had given the reporter a "no comment" but wanted me to know that neither he nor the marketing committee had asked for my resignation. Charlie just laughed at the official story when I met with him for a drink the next day.

Kenny and I said a quick good-bye. He thanked me for

what I'd done, "not for me, but for N-Y-R-A," and we shook hands. There were a few projects he wanted me to finish up, and he told me to go ahead and attend a couple of conferences where I had been scheduled to speak. NYRA would pay my expenses and keep me on the payroll and extend my medical benefits for a generous 90 days

Exactly 91 days later, I was sitting at home tuning up my speed figures when suddenly my left arm went numb. I had seen enough medical dramas to think "heart attack" without waiting for things to get worse, and two hours later I was having an angioplasty to open up a blocked artery. The procedure went perfectly and I was shot full of sedatives and moved to intensive care, where Robin was told I'd be fine but couldn't have visitors for a few days.

The second morning, I awoke in a fog and saw someone larger than Robin sitting in a chair across from my bed.

"Jesus Christ, pardnuh, you look like hell," Kenny said. "No wonder they said I couldn't come see you but you know I'm not much for rules and regulations. Anyway, don't worry about nothing. I told Robin we'll make sure you're covered for all this. Now get well and get your ass back to the betting windows. We at N-Y-R-A could use the money."

RETURNING TO FORM

W HEN I LEFT NYRA in January of 1997, I had just turned 40 and felt as if I was back to exactly where I had been when *The Racing Times* was shut down in February of 1992—freshly unemployed and with no prospects beyond getting reacquainted with the horses in New York so I could start betting them again.

The first time around, it had seemed like a grand gambling adventure. Now it seemed like my only option. I had been walking into the same racetracks for 16 years, just using a different door each time—to the press box as a reporter, to the Turf and Field Club as a gambler, or to the executive offices as a vice president. It would be fun to be back in action as a bettor now that Kenny's handcuffs had been removed, but I wanted to be more than a full-time customer living out his days chasing the pick six. There were still problems to be resolved and battles to be fought in the racing industry, and I wanted to be part of that process somehow, whether in a press box or a boardroom.

I decided to print up some business cards that read "Steven Crist—Consultant to the Parimutuel Industry." No one was consulting me about anything, but I had learned in my NYRA years that this was what every unemployed racing executive called himself while between jobs. If nothing else, it got you invited to speak at conferences, and reporters would phone you looking for sound bites, happy to quote a "consultant" rather than an "unemployed gambler."

I also had the notion that there might be room in the market for another racing publication. It had always seemed odd to me that the game lacked a weekly magazine for fans and bettors. The two trade journals, *The Blood-Horse* and *The Thoroughbred Times,* were weeklies devoted largely to breeding and auctions, aimed not at horseplayers but at the buyers and sellers of stallion seasons and sales yearlings.

Charlie Hayward and I had begun kicking around the idea of a new magazine even before I left NYRA. We had met at the racetrack 15 years earlier when I was starting out as a reporter and he was a young book salesman, but had lost track of each other until he joined the NYRA board in 1995 as part of a Dragone initiative to rejuvenate the trustee group. Charlie liked to say he had personally lowered the average net worth of the NYRA board members by a zero or two, but he was exactly the kind of new blood that Dragone was trying to mix in with the bluebloods.

Charlie had become a star in the world of book publishing,

rising through its ranks to be named the president and chief executive of the prestigious Little, Brown imprint in Boston. He was technically a horse owner, having had small shares with friends in some claimers over the years, but what he liked best about the game was going to the grandstand on the weekend in his shorts to enjoy some cold malt beverages and smoke a cigar or two while doping out the races.

Charlie left Little, Brown in 1996 and for a while tried to focus his energies on NYRA, volunteering to get the passive board to engage in some long-term planning and take a more modern view of the game in the era of simulcasting. Like a certain NYRA vice president he was getting friendly with, he found it a sometimes frustrating experience.

After I left NYRA, Charlie and I began to talk seriously about starting a racing magazine, or at least a newsletter. We felt we would make a good team at something. Charlie was a master salesman and he knew the business end of publishing as well as how to set up and administer a company. All we needed was the right project.

On March 3, 1997, Charlie and I opened our *Forms* at almost the same moment and were dialing each other's phone numbers practically before getting through a small news story on page 4: "Primedia to Sell DRF."

When we got on the phone, each of us knew why the other was calling. We had to get involved with this, but how? We were roughly $100 million short of the $100 million you probably would need in the bank just to get a copy of the sales prospectus. I had a discouraging mental image of two out-of-work horseplayers sitting in a grandstand, debating whether to buy the Lear jet or the yacht.

We split up to pursue leads. I would make a few calls within the racing industry to find out what I could, and Charlie would talk to some financial people he had met in the course of acquiring companies for Little, Brown.

My first call was to Alan Marzelli, the president of Equibase. He had seen the story too and said he had told his wife, "I wonder how long it's going to take for Steve to call."

I had two questions for him: Was Equibase going to bid on the *Form?* And if someone else bought it, would Equibase still make the data-collection deal with a new owner that the *Form* had turned down in 1992 and again when Alan and I were on the Equibase board in 1995?

No and yes. Equibase, he said, would not be a bidder. The company didn't have the capital for a major acquisition and was doing just fine competing with the *Form* through track programs. Besides, there might be antitrust issues if the industry-owned Equibase was both the sole collector and sole distributor of past-performance data. The best outcome, he thought, would be a new owner for the *Form* who would make a deal to use Equibase's data. If I were involved with that owner, he said, he was confident that he and I could make a data deal in about five minutes flat.

Charlie also had good news. He had talked to several people who bought and sold companies, and they didn't think the idea of our pursuing the *Form* was the craziest thing they had ever heard. We met with one of them, a media consultant named Stewart Nazarro, and told him the whole saga of *The Racing Times* and what had happened to the *Form* in the intervening years.

The *Form* had been sold by the Annenberg family to Rupert Murdoch's News Corporation for about $400 million in 1988, and by Murdoch to K-III (which now called itself Primedia) for about $250 million in 1991. We still hadn't seen any current financials, but the company had to be worth much less now, given that Equibase track programs had devastated *Form* sales over the last five years.

Meanwhile, the paper itself had become less and less essential. In its stodgiest days, the *Form* may have been dull and safe and painted a perpetually rosy picture of the game, but it had nevertheless been required reading for the sport's participants and its most serious customers. Now, though, its news coverage had taken a turn for the worse.

Primedia had responded to the loss of business not by improving the product but by cutting costs. The main operation had been moved from New Jersey to Phoenix, Arizona, hardly a major racing or media center but an employer-friendly state where you could pay lower salaries. Neil Cook and his page-production unit from *The Racing Times* had become the editors of the paper, and the editorial judgment had become tinged with a British-tabloid sensibility. Reporters regularly wrote fiery opinion columns on the same issues they were supposed to be covering objectively, blurring the line between straight news and editorial comment.

On the business side, declining sales and the changes wrought by simulcasting had shaken the *Form*'s greatest strength—its reliable availability, the critical importance of which I had learned at *The Racing Times*. To cut costs, Primedia had kept reducing print runs and eliminating sales outlets. Lifelong customers who had been buying the paper every morning at the same store suddenly found that it was sold out by 8:00 A.M. or that the store had been dropped from the delivery route altogether. Forced to pick up a track program instead, many found that they could handicap almost as well with it, and they didn't miss the editorial content that most had stopped reading anyway. The *Form* had the Beyer figures and a familiar look and feel but little else to compel anyone to spend $4 for a newspaper instead of $1.50 for a track program.

More than a year after the shutdown of *The Racing Times*, the *Form* had appropriated about half of the statistical innovations, and had done so in a way that still had me seething four years later. In a front-page story in April of 1993, the *Form* announced that it was introducing "new, expanded past performances" that had been conceived by the *Form's* "panel of editors" after months of grueling meetings—"innovations" such as the career box, sire of sire, expanded race conditions, and layoff lines.

The only acknowledgment of the source of these changes was an oblique comment that might have been read as a tip of the hat, but I took it as the grinding of a heel: "The new past performances," the story said, "are all substance."

I had written a furious and overblown letter of protest to Jack Farnsworth, the *Form's* chief executive and publisher, saying haughtily that "While buying a corpse certainly entitles you to pick the gold from its teeth, it does not mitigate the fraudulence of your claiming to have spun that gold yourself." Fortunately, I had always heeded a valuable piece of advice from my mother: When you write such a letter, sleep on it for 24 hours and then decide if you really want to mail it. A day later, I had decided not to give Farnsworth the satisfaction of my outrage and never sent the letter—a good decision, since he was now one of the people with whom we would be trying to do business.

The more Stewart listened to us talk about the *Form*, the more he insisted that we were the ideal buyers, not only because of my passion and Charlie's business expertise, but also because we held an ace—an Equibase deal. If we could pay Equibase $2 million a year for the data instead of spending

$5 million collecting it ourselves, that was an immediate $3 million a year upturn for the company.

The rule of thumb, he said, was to multiply any annual improvement by a factor of four to eight in order to determine how much value you were adding to the worth of the enterprise, so an Equibase deal was worth $12 million to $24 million to us as potential buyers. We could afford to offer that much more for the property than a bidder without such a deal in his back pocket, or perhaps that potential profit would make us the only bidder who could make a go of the enterprise.

I could grasp that kind of simple math, and as we began poring over financial statements and constructing a business plan, I found that a great deal of the mysterious world of high finance was nothing more than basic arithmetic that any competent horseplayer could do in his sleep. Revenue minus expenses equals profit, whether it's a $50 million company or a day at the track. A 15 percent return on investment is the same as getting $2.30 to show.

What I lacked was the jargon of the financial world. I spent an entire meeting with Stewart and his associates faking and nodding while everyone in the room was talking about improving the company's "E-bidder." It sounded like an electronic means of submitting a bid and I was too embarrassed even to ask Charlie what an E-bidder was. I bought a book called *How to Read Financial Statements* and finally figured out that "E-bidder" was actually EBITDA, an accounting acronym for "*e*arnings *b*efore *i*nterest, *t*axes, *d*epreciation, and *a*mortization." In other words, revenue minus expenses, or payoffs minus bets.

Stewart steered us through putting together a presentation for potential investors. He said the undertaking needed a code name that didn't include the words *Racing Form*, so we called it Project Alydar. In early April we presented it to Nancy Peretsman of Allen and Company, an investment-banking firm that I had heard of only because one of the owners, Herbert Allen, had a string of racehorses.

Nancy, who had been named one of the 50 most powerful women in American business by *Fortune* magazine, was a whirlwind deal-maker who spoke twice as quickly as anyone else in the room and could think even faster. She wrapped her mind around the *Form* deal immediately and told us it could be done. Allen and Company itself was not making such "small" investments, though, and what we needed was a venture-capital company to back us. She had two in mind, Boston Ventures and Alpine Capital, and she wanted to try them in that order.

A week later we met with Boston Ventures' Tony Bolland and Jamie Wilson, a pair of formal and meticulous Brits who specialized in working with management teams to develop media acquisitions. Their deals had included such well-known companies as *Billboard,* Mattel, Metromedia, and Motown. They came highly recommended not only by Nancy but also by the tabloid publisher who had wanted to buy *The Racing Times* before being threatened with the loss of KKR's cigarette advertising.

The Boston Ventures guys seemed to like us immediately, and after looking at the financials, Tony Bolland said that it could be "a very attractive deal in the $60 million range." I just nodded along with everyone else, still completely confused about where the $60 million would come from and how this all worked.

As I was able to piece it together, buying a company was sort of like buying a house. You had to come up with the equivalent of a down payment in actual cash, and you went out and borrowed the rest, just like getting a mortgage. So the idea was that Boston Ventures, if they went ahead, would put up $10 million to $15 million of their own money and borrow the rest from banks and other investors, paying off the loans out of profits.

The management team—Charlie and I and the key three or four executives we would hire—could gradually earn a small stake in the company if it performed well. Charlie and I would be expected to prove our commitment and belief by putting up our own "earnest money," maybe $250,000 to $500,000 each, for a minuscule initial ownership interest.

After the meeting, Nancy and Charlie told me how well it had gone and that things were looking good. That was great, I told them, but I would have a problem proving my "earnest-ness": I couldn't raise a sum of money with that many zeroes in it unless I was the sole winner of the next three-day carry-over at Aqueduct. Not to worry, they said: Boston Ventures would probably be happy to lend me the money at a reasonable rate of interest.

I wasn't doing anything particularly smart at the track while paying increasingly less attention to the game as the deal progressed, and my savings were running out. My NYRA medical benefits would be up in a week. I had been having some serious dental problems and needed three long sessions of massive periodontal surgery. When I told the dentist my coverage was about to expire, he said we should combine two of the scheduled sessions and he'd just give me some extra painkillers.

So two days after being told I was in such great position to complete a $60 million business deal, I was scheming to save $1,000 by getting a double dose of dental surgery before my coverage lapsed. It was the most agonizing afternoon of my life and I still don't believe it was a coincidence that 72 hours later I had my heart attack.

I was home from the hospital in just five days, but then I got *really* sick. Something went awry with the interaction of drugs I had been prescribed, and I spent more than a week in chemical chaos. Robin had to wake me to stagger to the living room for two minutes to watch Silver Charm win the Kentucky Derby.

The fog lifted a few days later and I slowly went back to work on the deal with a renewed sense of purpose. I hadn't seen a white light or had any epiphanies about mortality, but I had been overwhelmed by the number of people from my nine lives around the racetrack who had sought me out when word got around that I was laid up. I had always thought I had done an inadequate job of making and keeping friends, writing and handicapping in seclusion while others were building relationships or at least having people over for dinner, but now I saw there was something to the cliché that the people you work with become your family.

Everyone had the same three instructions for the patient. Get well. Start taking better care of yourself. And get this deal for the *Form* done.

CHARLIE HAD KEPT things moving during my illness. Primedia had engaged Morgan Stanley to conduct an auction for the property, but it had become clear that we were the only serious bidders and that $60 million was going to be an acceptable price. Getting the deal done boiled down to two things: convincing Boston Ventures to commit to going ahead, and executing the Equibase agreement.

Bolland and Wilson shared a favorite word: *comfort*. Every business assumption was challenged, dissected, and reassembled to provide them with a "comfort level." They hired one outside consultant after another—including separate experts in newspaper distribution, gambling trends, and system technology—so they could "get comfortable" with the industries in which the *Form* would be operating. Wilson's way of telling you that you had done or said something good was to say, "I take great comfort in hearing that."

The one thing they were uncomfortable about was the long-term health of horse racing. They repeatedly said they did not invest in "declining businesses," and we had to prove to them that racing was not a dying sport—at least not in the next five years, the time they typically held on to properties before selling them at a profit. They found little comfort in the general media depiction of racing as a game past its prime, surpassed by other sports as entertainment and dwarfed by casinos and lotteries as a form of gambling. Despite our optimism about the game, all they read and heard was that racing was beset by an aging fan base and declining attendance.

I had been hearing about the fan base since I had first come around the track and argued that this was a perpetual phenomenon rather than a new one. I was able to dig out columns from 50 years ago in trade publications bemoaning racing's relatively elderly crowd. It made sense that a game often played on weekdays and almost always during daylight hours, requiring both disposable time and disposable income, had never drawn many younger people. Nothing had changed except a modern fixation throughout the world of business that a younger demographic was always a desirable thing.

There was no denying that track attendance had been declining steadily for a decade, but we believed that this didn't really tell the whole story. Total national betting handle was actually creeping up a percent or two each year because existing players were investing more, now that there were up to

100 simulcast races a day to bet on instead of just nine or 10 live events.

We didn't need to increase racing's fan base to make a go of the *Form*. We just needed to slow the steady migration from *Forms* to track programs. Rather than dumbing-down the paper, we needed to raise it to the level where the serious customers would consider it a must-read, through better editorial content and with even more high-end statistics.

We gave our final presentation to the Boston Ventures board on June 19 and convinced them to move ahead. It was starting to seem real. All that was left was "due diligence"—two months of going through all the *Form*'s records and contracts—and wrapping up the Equibase deal. We spent most of July on the documents and by the time Saratoga opened it looked as if we might be taking over the *Form* by September 1.

Then the first draft of the Equibase contract arrived.

I had gone ahead and rented our usual house in Saratoga with what was left of my savings, certain that I would be in the chips again in a few weeks, but as I sat on the porch reading the contract it was like watching a horse with a 20-length lead slow to a crawl in deep stretch. I had assumed that this was going to be no more complicated than the one-page letter of intent we had already signed with Equibase to give BV some comfort, saying that we would turn over the *Form*'s database to Equibase, pay them to collect the information going forward, and have a perpetual license to use it in the newspaper. Marzelli and I had spent a year together on the Equibase board talking about what a "no-brainer" such an arrangement would be for an enlightened owner of the *Form*.

What I had now was a far more complex and restrictive document. We were $1 million a year apart on price, but that was the least of our problems. Equibase wanted to limit our ability to resell the data to their existing track-program clients, and also wanted to keep for itself the right to use the data as part of future electronic-wagering systems.

As if to play catch-up after years of ignoring off-track betting and emerging technology, the industry in general and The Jockey Club in particular had begun an infatuation with the possibilities of in-home wagering over the computer. Plans were being made for an industry-wide effort to package the top tracks' signals and get them into homes through cable or satellite television; somehow, this was going to save racing and generate up to $50 million a year for the industry. On this premise, a league office for the sport, the National Thoroughbred Racing Association, was in its formative stages.

The Boston Ventures guys were horrified when they saw the Equibase contract and the electronic restrictions. Charlie and I told them that we didn't think it was that big a deal, because given the industry's own track record, this electronic wonderland was odds-on to remain a pipe dream. On the off chance that it came to pass, we argued, people could continue to buy their data from us even if they were using an industry-owned betting system that featured Equibase data.

The arguments didn't matter. Boston Ventures had already spent more than $750,000 pursuing the acquisition and felt it was getting the rug pulled out from under it at the last minute. The level of discomfort on both sides increased when a routine filing of the proposed sale sparked some interest from the Department of Justice over the possible antitrust implications of a *Form*-Equibase deal. Equibase's lawyers became convinced that the Boston Ventures lawyers were trying to trick them into signing a contract that would later be annulled by the government, while Boston Ventures began to believe that Equibase was trying to cripple the *Form*'s ability to succeed and ultimately wanted to take over the whole information franchise.

Charlie and I were trying to soothe everyone and hold the deal together, but each meeting between Equibase and Boston Ventures was more disastrous than the last. As every sentence of the data contract turned into a battleground, Bolland and Wilson became certain that the support and cooperation we needed from the industry had at best been damaged and at worst had never been there at all.

I had to miss a key meeting on the morning of September 29. A few months earlier, I had agreed to leave for Tokyo that day to make a speech to Japanese track officials about American racing, and I had been looking forward to being introduced as one of the brand-new proprietors of the *Form*. Just before my flight left, I called Charlie, who told me there had been a name-calling, table-pounding blow-up. It had ended with Marzelli telling Bolland and Wilson that they should go ahead and keep using the *Form*'s own data and that he would see them in bankruptcy court in two years when Equibase would pick up the *Form* for $25 million or so.

Charlie said he was going to try to get everyone back to the table, and it was time to board the flight. When I checked into my Tokyo hotel 16 hours later, there was a faxed letter from Charlie at the front desk, saying that Boston Ventures had officially bowed out of the deal.

"I'm really sorry, Steve," his note ended, "because I know that together we could have made a great success of the *Form*."

WELCOME TO TOKYO. The deal was dead, the last seven months were up in smoke, and I would need every last yen of my speaking fee to cover the October bills when I got home. And I had 10 minutes to get ready for a dinner with Toru Shirai, the Tokyo publisher who had printed the Japanese edition of one of my books nine years earlier.

It was a long evening, but after the first bottle of sake I stopped caring if the food on my plate was still moving. We ended up back at his Tokyo office where we played a slick new horse-racing video game that was sweeping his nation, and I began wondering if there might be career opportunities importing Japanese toys. I delivered my speech the next day, restraining myself from making any gratuitous remarks about the perfidy of the American racing establishment and practitioners of law.

When I got home, I was in denial that the quest for the *Form* had ended. There had to be a way to put the deal back together. It had been thoroughly researched, the buyer and seller were happy with the financial terms, and everything was ready to go. It just seemed insane that personality clashes and stubborn lawyering could wipe all that out.

Even Primedia offered to help. The *Form's* owners were almost as disappointed as we were that the sale was off, since they had no other buyers and were eager to get rid of a company they neither understood nor liked. Primedia officials urged us to go find another equity source and even suggested they might finance the debt.

Boston Ventures was still willing to move ahead with a transaction if the industry would remove Marzelli as the head of Equibase, but that was not going to happen. Marzelli had taken some heat from his board when the deal came apart, but had convinced them and himself that Bolland and Wilson were as diabolical as they thought him to be.

"I'm frankly glad the deal fell through," he told me two weeks after I got back from Tokyo. "*DRF* has got to fall into industry hands."

Charlie and I had little interest in being part of an industry-owned *Daily Racing Form*. The whole point of the undertaking was to make the *Form* the customers' paper and an independent voice, not to mislead the public while shilling for the industry. It would be as if the federal government owned *The Washington Post*.

We spent another three weeks meeting with various bankers and investors, but everyone seemed to think there had to be something wrong with the deal since it had already fallen apart once. It was getting difficult to convince people that Equibase and the *Form* were going to walk hand in hand into a bright future together when we hadn't even been able to execute a simple data license.

I could tell Charlie's enthusiasm was waning and he finally told me he was done chasing. He said he would help me in any way if I could get a deal going again, but that he didn't have the stomach for this anymore. I was disappointed but I understood. For me, getting the *Form* was a passion play with a long history, and a chance to right the wrongful ending of *The Racing Times*. For Charlie, the *Form* would have been the perfect job, combining his skills and his favorite hobby, but it was a business opportunity rather than a personal crusade. How could I blame him for wanting to get back to publishing books and enjoying his Saturdays at the races?

Without Charlie as my partner, Allen and Company lost any interest in finding new equity sources and Nancy Peretsman advised me to go ask the *Form* to give me a job. That was about as likely as peace in the Middle East, but over the next two months I did keep talking to people at Primedia and

Morgan Stanley. Much as they didn't like me in general and were angry that the sale had been called off, they also knew that no one else really wanted the property.

Business was worse than ever, and in December Primedia announced that they were taking a $150 million write-off on the *Form*, effectively admitting they had overpaid for the property and devalued it. They also said that the *Form* was officially off the market pending some changes. In December I met with Jack Farnsworth at Primedia, where the walls were decorated with framed covers of the company's successful soap-opera and hunting magazines but there wasn't a *Form* on display.

Farnsworth told me the imminent changes at the *Form* would consist of two things: a round of serious cost-cutting, and a data deal between the *Form* and Equibase. He said everyone now realized an Equibase agreement would increase the *Form*'s value and that no one would think about buying the property without one in place.

Farnsworth added that Primedia still considered me the likeliest eventual buyer, and that I would be the first person to get a prospectus in March or April when the property went back on the market. That was sort of nice to hear, but pretty hollow. I had no partner and no backers, and it sounded as if the price of the property would be going up.

Meanwhile, I was scrambling to pay the bills and borrowing from predatory loan sharks—not shady characters at the track, but credit-card companies, who kept sending me new and bigger cash advances. It was the only time in my life that I felt like a compulsive gambler, and I wasn't even playing the races anymore. Had getting the *Form* become a ruinous obsession? I was no longer a confident bettor, coolly seeking propositions where I would be getting the best of the odds. I was playing an unfamiliar game with stakes I couldn't afford, borrowing one chip after another to stay at the table. At least I was betting on myself.

I had just about given up trying to find backers when a couple of friends led me to ones I had forgotten about entirely. Irwin Cohen, who had suffered through the failed Boston Ventures deal with us, had a lifelong friend, David Heinemann, who was buying and selling software companies. David suggested we try a company named Alpine Capital, because one of the principals, Richard Goldstein, had grown up in Queens with Irwin and David.

The name Alpine rang a bell and I wondered whether I had already pitched them; by now I had lost track of all the institutional investors we had chased. I found in my notes that they were the next company Nancy Peretsman was going to call if Boston Ventures had not been interested.

Alpine's principals—Richard, his partner, Bruce Greenwald, and their chairman, Ed Aboodi—had come out of Time-Warner, where Aboodi had been the company's deal-maker, with Richard his legal expert and Bruce the finance wizard. They had formed Alpine to do their own transactions, and described themselves as "opportunistic investors," meaning they would do a good deal regardless of the industry. Their investments ranged from upscale child-care facilities and stadium-seating movie theaters to cellular telephones in China and budget motels in the Midwest.

We met with Richard and Bruce, and they were immediately intrigued. They were the first people not to look at us sideways after hearing the story of the first deal's blowup. Richard understood how a good deal could be destroyed by a temperamental lawyer because he was one.

They liked the idea of owning the *Form*, a sexier property than their others, and took comfort that Boston Ventures had done so much work and come within one contract of making the deal. (To their credit, Alpine invited Boston Ventures back in, but Bolland and Wilson declined, saying they simply couldn't trust Equibase, and Alpine later paid them a fee for our use of their due-diligence reports.)

They also thought the idea that the *Form* would sell for more in the wake of an Equibase deal was absurd. The $60 million Boston Ventures bid had included another small property owned by the *Form*, so $55 million had been the offer for the *Form* alone. I was afraid it would now command $65 million or more, but the Alpine guys insisted that $40 million to $45 million would get it done.

The next few months were like reliving the Boston Ventures deal—reviewing documents and contracts, making presentations, and proving the case that a *Form* acquisition made sense all over again. Charlie was back in the fold in spirit, insisting he was acting only as a friend and consultant but doing as much work on the transaction as he had the first time around. As we pitched bankers for financing, it made a much better impression to have a clean-shaven, accomplished businessman such as Charlie on stage to balance the mustachioed horseplayer and journalist.

Early in April, the *Form* announced it had signed a data deal with Equibase. When we got hold of it, it was frustrating to see that all the points of earlier contention had been removed and it was a document that we and Boston Ventures would have signed in a minute. I was about to find out why things had gotten so cozy between the one-time mortal enemies.

The day that Primedia announced that the *Form* was for sale again, I called Marzelli and had a moment of déjà vu. It had been 13 months since that day I had phoned him to see if Equibase was going to make a run at the *Form*. Here we go again, I told him, and just for a laugh I asked him the same first question: So, was Equibase going to bid on the *Form*?

This time, there was a long silence. Then Marzelli broke the news: "We're going after it ourselves."

Maybe I should have seen it coming, since Marzelli had told me six months earlier he thought the *Form* should end up in the industry's hands. I was sure we were sunk, and the only question was whether I would want to be part of an industry-owned *Form*, not that I'd been invited.

That came a week later, when Marzelli summoned me to his office for a polite but vaguely ominous conversation.

"We would prefer that you not pursue this acquisition," he said. There could be a role for me, probably involving moving to Phoenix to edit an industry-owned paper, and the best thing I could do for everyone involved would be to convince Alpine to step aside.

"We" was more than just Equibase. Marzelli had been working with the *Form's* management, which had found a venture-capital group to provide the bulk of the financing; in return, they would continue to run the operation. As for the equity, The Jockey Club and Equibase were going to put up their own money and had asked several major track operators, including NYRA and Churchill Downs, to join them as partners.

I walked the two blocks from Equibase's offices to Alpine's, ready to apologize for having wasted their time and money, but when I got there and told them what we were up against, Richard and Bruce were hardly fazed. So there was another bidder. There usually was. They'd take their chances on me and Charlie against an industry that, from everything they had learned, couldn't organize a two-car funeral. With the Equibase deal in place, it would still be to the industry's advantage to see the *Form* survive, and they said not to be so sure we were up against a united front.

Charlie, who was still a NYRA trustee, had been surprised at a recent board meeting when "*Daily Racing Form*" had turned up on the agenda. Kenny had told the assembled trustees, including Jockey Club chairman Dinny Phipps, that The Jockey Club had asked NYRA to kick in $1 million and it was under consideration. Charlie had then explained his involvement with our competing bid, and several of the NYRA trustees had wondered aloud afterward why NYRA would be opposing us.

A week later I saw Kenny at the track and he rushed over and pulled me aside.

"Why in hell is The Jockey Club trying to get in the way of you and Charlie?" he asked. "I told Phipps and that gang they didn't have any business running a newspaper but I don't know if they'll listen to me. It's the stupidest goddamn idea I've heard in a long time. I can think of a lot better things N-Y-R-A can do with a million bucks. Don't give up, pardnuh."

Why indeed was the industry now bidding? Had Equibase deliberately blown up the first transaction because they had decided it was a better deal for them? Had I been the pawn in a long conspiracy to put the *Form* in industry hands?

During the Boston Ventures deal, I had always thought we had enjoyed an advantage over any potential non-industry bidder because our group alone knew the value of an Equibase data deal and had the connections to pull one off. Now, it seemed, the edge had gone to the other side. The *Form* had to be worth more to the industry than to us because it could control the entire competitive landscape. Was the plan now for the industry to discontinue past-performance programs and make everyone buy a *Form*, re-creating the old Annenberg monopoly? How could we possibly make a competitive bid against that lucrative scenario?

A newspaper reporter lives by his sources, insiders who tell him what's happening behind the scenes, but in this case we had too many sources and no sense of which ones to trust. Every day, Charlie, Irwin, and I would each get calls from people who worked at the *Form*, Primedia, or somewhere in the racing industry, passing on the latest rumors. We would hear that bidders were raising their prices—but was that just Primedia trying to spur us to a higher number? We would hear that one track or another was ponying up its $1 million to help the industry's bid—but was that just an attempt to scare us out of the chase? Even our friends inside the *Form* who were trying to help us were being fed disinformation by *Form* management, which was now aligned with the industry group.

Business writers for the New York papers kept coming up with additional interested bidders. It was supposedly a five-way race now, including not only our group and the industry's but also Hachette Filipacchi, a New York-based media conglomerate; John Harris, a prominent horse owner with a family fortune in California farmland behind him; and Everett Novak, who raced horses as the New Farm with the money he had made from licensing the rights to an annoying purple dinosaur named Barney.

Three days before the Belmont Stakes, we made our bid. Alpine had screened out all the rumors and held to the low end of its valuation of the property, submitting a bid of $40,250,000 just in case someone else offered exactly $40 million. I feared we would come up short, but this was what these guys did for a living and I had no choice but to trust them. We had grown to like one another, but they weren't going to over-pay for the property to fulfill my personal mission.

It was enough. Only one other bid was submitted: $35 million by the industry group, a figure so low, given their ability to control the market, that it gave some credence to Marzelli's subsequent explanation of his approach to the whole transaction. He said that Primedia had literally begged him to bid because they simply didn't believe I could pull off a deal. Marzelli maintains to this day that he really didn't care which one of us got the property so long as no one else did.

This time I took nothing for granted until the "Official" sign was posted. Negotiating the actual purchase agreement with Primedia took the better part of two months, and Richard Goldstein and the legal team fought over every comma. Each time there was a disagreement, I feared the deal would fall through again. I had spent more than a year imagining the business and editorial team I wanted to put together but I couldn't offer anyone a job. One grouchy lawyer on either side could put me back at square one.

We finally got there on August 14. I spent all day signing papers and at 5:00 P.M. got in a car with Robin and Irwin to drive to Saratoga, where we would announce the transaction the next day. I fell into a deep sleep and woke up as we were pulling up to a restaurant where Charlie, Marzelli, and *Form* and Equibase officials were waiting for us to join them at a celebratory dinner.

It was going to be interesting to see who reached for the check. We had won the auction but Equibase had won its own seven-year battle to become the game's sole data collector. Marzelli graciously picked up the tab and I didn't argue. After all, the *Form* was now his biggest customer.

Later that night, Irwin, Robin, and I ended up on the patio

of the Gideon Putnam, the last of Saratoga's grand hotels, savoring a day we had thought would never come. It had been six and a half years since the shutdown of *The Racing Times* and we finally felt entitled to raise our glasses one last time with a toast we could never use again: "Substance over Form."

IT WAS TEMPTING to conclude this book on that August evening, and not just because everyone likes a happy ending. Everything that has happened since is the unfinished story of an ongoing enterprise, and a personal memoir of what led up to it probably should not conclude with what could be construed as a corporate infomercial by a current employee.

Still, nobody likes a story with too many loose ends. So by way of brief epilogue, rather than a thorough accounting, here is some of what happened next.

I had my first official business meeting the day after the acquisition when I sat down for a cup of coffee with Tim Smith, the commissioner of the newly formed National Thoroughbred Racing Association. He wanted to know what his group could do to establish some credibility with the customers, and I told him a good first step might be to recognize a horseplayer at the annual Eclipse Awards dinner along with the equine and human champions.

This discussion led to the creation of the DRF/NTRA National Handicapping Championship, a nationwide series of over 50 horseplaying contests that now draws 40,000 entrants a year. The winner is honored as the Horseplayer of the Year at the Eclipse dinner, and so far they've all been *Form* users.

If I had learned anything from *The Racing Times*, it was not to overwhelm the readers with a bunch of changes to the familiar running lines. Since 1998, the *Form* has rolled out more than two dozen changes to the past performances, but they have come slowly, to get readers used to one enhancement before introducing another. These have included Tomlinson Ratings, a popular pedigree-based figure intended to predict success on grass and over sloppy tracks, and Trainer Form, a set of race-specific trainer statistics.

Two months after the acquisition, we relaunched the *Form* with a party at the All Star Café in Manhattan, where we introduced the paper's new look, talent, and management.

I had years to reorganize and restaff the *Form* in my mind. We unveiled a newsier front page and a brand-new page 2, which was a daily leader board for the sport and featured a ranking of the top horses in each division by Mike Watchmaker, whom I had hired away from the line-making job at NYRA to be our national handicapper.

Pages 3 and 4 were hard news, much of it written by either Jay Privman, whom I had recruited as our national correspondent; Matt Hegarty, an outstanding young reporter who agreed to relocate from Phoenix to New York; or David Grening, the top local beat writer, who left the *New York Post* to join us. The *Form*'s reportorial staff, slashed to a handful in the Primedia days, is now a robust unit of new hires and the best of the old guard, a team that also includes Steve Andersen, Glenye Cain, Marcus Hersh, Karen Johnson, Marty McGee, Mary Rampellini, Bill Tallon, and Mike Welsch.

Page 5 was a new daily editorial page, though I had decided early on that the *Form* would not run unsigned editorials that pretended to be the official position of the newspaper. Instead, we would have four dedicated and regular columnists, expressing their own opinions with no interference from management or ownership: Joe Hirsch, who at the age of 75 is writing better than ever; Jay Hovdey, whose eloquent dispatches from his California base have given the paper a long-overdue bicoastal balance; Andrew Beyer, who requires no further introduction; and, especially since we didn't have to pay him extra, a former *New York Times* racing writer who had badly missed having a place to air his grumpy opinions.

We had arranged with *The Washington Post* to run the columns Beyer writes for them, frequently on a same-day basis, since the papers are hardly in competition. As famous as Andy had become as an author of books and through the Beyer Speed Figures, his excellent columns had rarely been seen by racing people outside the Baltimore-Washington area.

We also established a daily page devoted to handicapping, which includes columns not only from top *Form* handicappers such as Brad Free, Steve Klein, and Dave Litfin but also from outside contributors including Joe Cardello, Dick Jerardi, and Lauren Stich.

The idea to run Andy's columns came from our new executive editor—Rich Rosenbush, who still complains that I singled Turkoman against Groovy in that 1986 pick six. Rich had passed on *The Racing Times*, but this time he was willing to make the jump, and resigned his post as deputy sports editor at *The New York Times* to join us. Victor Mather, our star copy editor at *The Racing Times*, had gone on to the sports desk at the other *Times* and came along with Rich as his deputy.

The editorial executive team was completed by Irwin and by Duke Dosik, who had been valiantly getting the paper out in Phoenix every day while Primedia had been cutting his resources to the bone. Duke was one of the 10 out of 54 Phoenix employees who came to New York when we relocated the headquarters to lower Manhattan early in 2000.

One of Irwin's first projects was to revive *The American Racing Manual*, the 1,500-page yearly almanac that Primedia had stopped publishing in 1995. Irwin hired Steve Davidowitz, whose book had been my first comprehensive guide to the game, to edit and improve the *Manual* each year.

Katherine Wilkins, whom I'd first met at the Wembley dog races with George White in 1990, had gone from *The Racing Times* to the *Form* in 1992, rising to become the vice president of marketing before leaving the company in frustration when Primedia declined to give her any resources to create a *Form* business on the Internet. Katherine now came back to the *Form* two weeks after the acquisition and, working with Dave Ward, who had created my personal past performances when I was betting in the Turf and Field years, launched a world-class website with online past performances.

Katherine became the first senior executive to leave the new *Form* when she moved to Baltimore in 2001 and married Joe DeFrancis, the owner of the Maryland Jockey Club. She remains a consultant to the company and has been ably succeeded by Mandy Minger, who began her career as Katherine's assistant at *The Racing Times*.

One of Mandy's responsibilities is overseeing the *Form*'s television commercials, which are produced by Steve Nagler, part of the fledgling pick-six partnership of 1985 and the producer of many of racing's best telecasts. Another is staging handicapping seminars each morning of the Saratoga meeting at Siro's restaurant, where Harvey Pack is the host and Andy Serling is among the regular guests.

Bill Dow, the *Form*'s president during the Primedia years, was the one top executive from the old regime we wanted to keep, and he kindly stayed on for more than a year as president and has remained a valued adviser. His successor as president—

the best possible person, but one I had never expected to come aboard full-time after the first deal blew up—volunteered for the job six months after the acquisition.

Charlie had set up a consulting business called Hayward Publishing Ventures and the *Form* had been his first client. He had been my confidante and principal adviser as I attempted to impersonate being a chief executive, and after a year of that he asked me to think about bringing him in full-time when Bill retired. I told him I didn't need any time to think about it and welcomed him back as the partner he had been since the first day of the venture.

The *Form*'s "E-bidder" earnings, once over $40 million a year, had fallen below $8 million in 1997, but have been between $10.2 million and $11.5 million in the four full years since the acquisition. The annual double-digit circulation declines of the 1990's have slowed to a relative trickle even as track attendance has continued to fall. The *Form* has increased its share of that market while replacing newspaper revenue with Internet sales and new products such as DRF Press books and a revamped charts publication, *National Simulcast Weekly*.

Alpine usually sells companies in less time than it has held on to this one, but is in no hurry to let go of what has been a solid and successful investment. The $34 million it borrowed in 1998 is being paid off well ahead of schedule.

As for me, three and a half years of overseeing daily business affairs proved more than enough. I had wanted the *Form* to be the best possible newspaper and had enjoyed every creative moment of the undertaking, but I found those moments growing fewer and fewer as my time instead was dominated by contract negotiations, administrative details, and the reasonable but relentless demands of the owners to improve profits.

I was lucky enough to have a partner who enjoyed pure business more than I did and was better at it, too. Early in 2002, I fulfilled Allan Dragone's prophecy that there was only one job that really suited me in the corporate world and became the *Form's* chairman. Charlie succeeded me as the chief executive officer, the role we had initially anticipated since the first day Primedia put the *Form* up for sale. At this writing, he has yet to ask any employees to dance the Macarena.

As I was finishing this manuscript, an invitation arrived in the mail for the 25th reunion of the Harvard Class of 1978. Unfortunately, the university did not consult a racing calendar before scheduling the festivities for the same day as the 2003 Belmont Stakes. Since it eventually worked out pretty well the first time around, I think I'll be choosing the racetrack over academia again.

ACKNOWLEDGMENTS

In addition to those whose names appear in this manuscript, I wish to thank the following friends and colleagues for their personal kindness and professional assistance during the various events chronicled in this book: Kathy Billanti, Peter Callahan, Bob Fierro, Rob Fleder, Jim Gluckson, Jim Kostas, Mike Kravchenko, Marty Lieberman, Bennett Liebmann, Noel Michaels, Gary Nelson, and Jack Wilson. Additionally, there are too many other people to mention whose work for *The Racing Times* and *Daily Racing Form* have helped to make the greatest game ever invented even better.

I am especially appreciative of the encouragement I received from a circle of readers who critiqued the manuscript at various stages. For their time and advice, I am grateful to Irwin Cohen, Scott Cooper, Judith Crist, Dean Keppler, Mandy Minger, Tim O'Leary, Kurt Paseka, Rich Rosenbush, Mike Watchmaker, and Katherine Wilkins.

Charlie Hayward deserves special thanks for pushing me to write the book I really wanted to after a few false starts. Chris Donofry's cover and jacket designs gave the book an ideal look.

As always, my greatest thanks are due to Robin Foster, who

not only lived through most of this story as it happened but also dissected, edited, and improved the manuscript as it developed.

May 2003